Vol. LXVIII

No. 5

Overland Monthly

AN ILLUSTRATED MAGAZINE OF THE WEST

CONTENTS FOR MAY 1917

NOTICE.—Contributions to the Overland Monthly should be typewritten, accompanied by full
return postage and with the author's name and address plain written in upper corner of first
page. Manuscripts should never be rolled.

The publisher of the Overland Monthly will not be responsible for the preservation or mail
miscarriage of unsolicited contributions and photographs.

Issued Monthly. $1.20 per year in advance. Ten cents per copy. Back numbers not over three
months old, 25 cents per copy. Over three months old, 50 cts. each. Postage: To Canada, 2 cts.;
Foreign, 4 cts.

Published by the OVERLAND MONTHLY COMPANY, San Francisco, California.

259 MINNA STREET.

**Limited Edition of
1000**

Copyright © 1987
by
Star Rover House

Library of Congress Catalog Number

ISBN 0-932458-37-8

Star Rover House
at
Jack London Heritage House
1914 Foothill Blvd.
Oakland, California 94606

Meeting the Universal Need

In the high passes of the mountains, accessible only to the daring pioneer and the sure-footed burro, there are telephone linemen stringing wires.

Across bays or rivers a flat-bottomed boat is used to unreel the message-bearing cables and lay them beneath the water.

Over the sand-blown, treeless desert a truck train plows its way with telephone material and supplies.

Through dense forests linemen are felling trees and cutting a swath for lines of wire-laden poles.

Vast telephone extensions are progressing simultaneously in the waste places as well as in the thickly populated communities.

These betterments are ceaseless and they are voluntary, requiring the expenditure of almost superhuman imagination, energy and large capital.

In the Bell organization, besides the army of manual toilers, there is an army of experts, including almost the entire gamut of human labors. These men, scientific and practical, are constantly inventing means for supplying the numberless new demands of the telephone using public.

AMERICAN TELEPHONE AND TELEGRAPH COMPANY
AND ASSOCIATED COMPANIES

One Policy   *One System*   *Universal Service*

SAN FRANCISCO'S
HOTEL PLAZA

HOTEL PLAZA
SAN FRANCISCO
(UNION SQUARE)

European Plan
$1.50 up

American Plan
$3.50 up

Our Main Cafe
Being Operated
on the a la
Carte and Table
d'Hote Plans.

Special Rooms
for Banquets and
Private Parties.

To Jack London

By George Sterling

Oh, was there ever face, of all the dead,
In which, too late, the living could not read
A mute appeal for all the love unsaid—
A mute reproach for careless word and deed?

And now, dear friend of friends, we look on thine,
To whom we could not give a last farewell,—
On whom, without a whisper or a sign,
The deep, unfathomable Darkness fell.

Oh! Gone beyond us, who shall say how far?
Gone swiftly to the dim Eternity,
Leaving us silence, or the words that are
To sorrow as the foam is to the sea.

Unfearing heart, whose patience was so long!
Unresting mind, so hungry for the truth!
Now hast thou rest, O gentle one and strong,
Dead like a lordly lion in its youth!

Farewell! although thou know not, there alone.
Farewell! although thou hear not in our cry
The love we would have given had we known.
Ah! And a soul like thine—how shall it die?

Entrance to the present Jack London farm residence, Valley of the Moon.

Sizing up new prize short horn stock, Jack London farm.

Cruising up the wide reaches of the San Joaquin River, California. (1914.)

OVERLAND

MONTHLY

Founded 1868

BRET HARTE

VOL. LXIX   San Francisco, May, 1917   No. 5

The late Jack London.

A Study of Jack London in His Prime

By

George Wharton James

A T THE beginning of the year (1912), Jack London was thirty-six years old. In those thirty-six years he has managed to crowd the experiences of a country lad on a farm, a street newsboy, a schoolboy, a member of a street-gang, a boy Socialist street orator, a voracious reader of books from the public library, an oyster bed patrol to catch oyster pirates, a longshoreman, a salmon fisher, able to sail any kind of a rude vessel on the none too smooth waters of San Francisco Bay, a sailor before the mast, seal hunting in the Behring Sea, a member of the Henry Clay debating club, a strenuous advocate of the Socialist Labor party, a student in the Oakland high school, a freshman in the University of California, a gold seeker in the Klondike, a driver of wolf-dogs over the snows of the frozen North, stricken with scurvy, one of three who embarked in an open boat and rode nineteen hundred miles in nineteen days down the Yukon to the Behring Sea, an orphan compelled to support his widowed mother and a nephew, a short story writer, a war correspondent, a

On the Snark's lifeboat, Solomon Islands, South Seas, 1908. Mrs. London is laughing at the amateur photographer's efforts to get a "good" picture.

novelist, an essayist, the owner and worker of a magnificent estate of over a thousand acres, the builder of the "Snark," which he navigated through the Pacific and the South Seas to Australia, and taught himself navigation while in actual charge of the "Snark" on the high seas; the planter of two hundred thousand eucalyptus trees on his estate; the engineer and constructor of miles of horse trails or bridle-paths through the trees, on the hill-sides and in the canyons of his estate; and now the builder of one of the most striking, individualistic, comfortable and endurable home mansions ever erected on the American continent. He has a list of thirty-one books to his credit, seven of them novels, one of them being one of the most popular books of its time and still selling by the thousand, another a book of social studies of the underworld of London that ranks with General Booth's "Submerged Tenth," Jacob Riis' "How the Other Half Lives," William T. Stead's "If Christ Came to Chicago," and surpasses them all in the vivid intensity

Aboard the "Roamer," in the confluences of the Sacramento and San Joaquin River, California (1915).

of its descriptions and the fierce passion for the downtrodden that it displays. His "War of the Classes," "The Iron Heel," and "Revolution," are bold and fearless presentations of his views on present-day social conditions, and what they are inevitably leading to, unless the leaders of the capitalistic class become more human and humane in dealing with the working classes. His "Before Adam," one of the best and most comprehensive of books on authropology, whether written by English, French, German or American, sets before the reader a clear and scientifically deduced conception of the upgrowth of the human race prior to the historic era when Adam and Eve appear.

His books have been translated into German, French, Swedish, Norwegian, Italian, Spanish and Russian, and wherever men think and talk and read, Jack London and his stories, his novels, his social theories are talked about, praised, abused, lauded and discussed. In Sweden he is the most popular foreign author. There Cali-

Jack London and Mrs. London aboard the U. S. S. Kilpatrick at Galveston, Texas, at the time that vessel sailed to Vera Cruz, Mexico, with General Funston and troops to handle the Mexican disturbances. Spring of 1914. London was acting as a war correspondent should trouble ensue.

fornia is known as Jack-London-Land.

Who, then, shall say that he has not lived? For good or evil he has made a profound impression upon his generation. Hundreds of thousands of words have been written, pro and con, about him and his work by critics of every school, country and type. Thousands buy and read his books and swear by him and his ideas; other thousands borrow and read and fiercely assail him.

Hence it seems to me it cannot fail to be more than usually interesting to take a close look at the man, seen through the eyes of one who is proud to call him friend, and who thinks he knows and understands him as well as any other living man.

One day while being favored by Luther Burbank to watch him at work in his "proving gardens," he explained that often one particular seed out of a batch grown under exactly the same conditions would develop into something so much ahead of the others as to be startling in its advancement. To watch for and capture these naturally developed and superior types was one of the most interesting and important phases of his great work.

Remembering this, and recalling London's vast and varied achievements with his rude early environment, I asked him one day: "Where did you come from? What are you the product of?" and here is his answer:

"Have you ever thought that in ten generations of my ancestors 1,022 people happened to concentrate in some fashion on the small piece of protoplasm that was to eventuate in me. All

Mrs. Jack London on a morning ride over the Valley of the Moon ranch.

the potentialities of these 1,022 people were favorable in my direction. I was born normal, healthy in body and mind. Many a life has been ruined by inheriting a tendency to a weak stomach, or liver, or lungs. In my case all were perfectly strong and vigorous. Then, too, you know that in a row of beans, all grown from the same seed, you will find one pod that surpasses all the others, and in that pod one bean that you may call 'the king bean.' It is so in humanity. All the accidents of environment favor the particular bean; they all favored me. Most people look upon the conditions of my early life as anything but favorable, but as I look back I am simply amazed at my chances, at the way opportunity has favored me. As a child I was very much alone. Had I been as other children, 'blessed' with brothers and sisters and plenty of playmates, I should have been mentally occupied, grown up as the rest of my class grew, become a laborer and been content. But I was alone. Very much so. This fostered contemplation. I well remember how I used

to look upon my mother. To me she was a wonderful woman with all power over my destiny. She had wisdom and knowledge, as well as power in her hands. Her word was my law. But one day she punished me for something of which I was not guilty. The poor woman had a hard life, and all her energies were spent in chasing the dollar that she might feed and clothe us, and she was worn out, nervous, irritable and therefore disinclined to take the time and energy necessary to investigate. So I was punished unjustly. Of course I cried and felt the injustice. Now, had I had companions, it would not have been long before I should have found them, or they me, and we should have engaged in some fun or frolic, and my attention would have been diverted. I should soon have 'laughed and forgot.' But it was not so. I thought, and thought, and thought, and my brooded thought soon incubated. I began to see differently. I began to measure. I saw that my mother was not as large as I had thought. Her infallibility was destroyed. She had seen all there

Jack London enjoying himself among his guests after doing his regular morning stunt of one thousand words in one of his popular stories.

was to see. Her knowledge was limited, and therefore she was unjust. I can well remember that I absolved her from any deliberate intention to hurt me, but henceforth I decided for myself as to the right and wrong of things.

"This contemplative spirit was fed by the accidents of the environment of childhood. I was born in San Francisco January 12, 1876, and for the first three and a half years lived in Oakland. Then my father took a truck farm (which is now a pottery) in Alameda, and I was there until I was seven years old. It was on my birthday that we moved. I can remember the picture as if it were but yesterday. We had horses and a farm wagon, and onto that we piled all our household belongings, all hands climbing up on the top of the load, and with the cow tied behind, we moved 'bag and baggage' to the coast in San Mateo County, six miles beyond Colina. It was a treeless bleak, barren and foggy region, yet as far as I was concerned, fate favored me. The only other people of the neighborhood were Italians and Irish. Ours was the only 'American' family. I had no companions. I went to the regular, old-fashioned country school, where three or four of us sat on the same bench, and were 'licked' as regularly as could be, 'good or bad.' My spirit of contemplation was fostered here, for I had no companions. I was a solitary and lonely child. Yet I was a social youngster, and always got along well with other children. I was healthy, hearty, normal and therefore

One of the last photographs taken of Jack London, 1916. He is seated in his study, reading part of the manuscript of one of the stories which was later contributed to this issue of Overland Monthly.

— Photo by Louis J. Stellmann.

happy, but I can now see that I lived a dual life. My outward life was that of the everyday poor man's son in the public school: rough and tumble, happy go lucky, jostled by a score, a hundred, rough elements. Within myself I was reflective, contemplative, apart from the kinetic forces around me.

"From here we moved, in less than a year, to Livermore, where I lived until I was nine years old. We had a rude kind of a truck farm, and I was the chore boy. How I hated my life there. The soil had no attractions for me. I had to get out early in the frosty mornings and I suffered from chilblains. Everything was squalid and sordid, and I hungered for meat, which I seldom got. I took a violent prejudice—nay, it was almost a hatred—to country life at this time, that later I had to overcome. All this tended to drive me into myself and added to my inward powers of contemplation.

"Then we moved to Oakland, where my real, active life began. I had to fish for myself."

Certainly he had if the following story, related by Ninetta Payne, the aunt and foster-mother of Charmian, his wife, be true:

"After school hours he sold newspapers on the streets, and not infrequently did battle to establish his right to route. An instance of the kind, told by an old neighbor of the Londons, is illustrative not only of Jack's grit and courage at thirteen, but of a certain phlegm and philosophic justice in his father. Jack had borne innumerable affronts from a sixteen year old boy until patience was exhausted and he resolved to fight it out. Accordingly at their next encounter the two fell to blows, Jack, cool and determined, as one predestined to conquer, and his antagonist swelling with the surface pride and arrogance of the bully. For more than two hours they stuck to it manfully, neither winning a serious advantage over the other.

The neighbor watcher thought it time to put a stop to the pummeling and ran to the London cottage, where she found the old man sunning himself on the doorstep.

" 'O Mr. London,' she cried, 'Jack's been fighting for hours! Do come and stop it!'

"He composedly returned: 'Is my boy fighting fair?'

" 'Yes, sir, he is.'

"He nodded, his pleased eyes twinkling. 'An' t'other one—is *he* fighting fair?'

" 'Yes—leastwise it looks so.'

" 'Well, let 'em alone. There don't seem no call to interfere.'

"That this placidity did not argue indifference was seen by the father's appearing a few minutes later on the field of action. He did nothing, however; only pulled steadily at his pipe and looked on, one of a motley ring of spectators. Jack's opponent was getting winded and bethought him of a subterfuge. He gave a blow and then threw himself on the ground, knowing that Jack would not hit him when he was down. The latter saw his little game, and when it was thrice repeated, struck low, with a telling punch on the chin of his falling adversary.

"There was a yell of 'Foul blow!' from the two younger brothers of the vanquished pugilist, and the older, an overgrown boy of fifteen, sprang red-hot into the circle and demanded satisfaction. Jack, panting and holding to his swollen wrist (that last blow of his had strained the tendons), pranced into position, and fired back the answer: 'Come on! I'll lick you, too!'

"It was observed that his father forgot to smoke during the spirited tussle that ensued, though he said never a word, even when Jack, dripping gore and sweat, drew off victorious from his prostrate foe, only to face the third brother, a lad of his own age. Him he downed with a single thrust of his fist, for his blood was up and he felt cordial to himself and invincibly confident in his strength to overcome a host of irate brothers.

"Then it was that John London,

bright of eye and smiling, took a gentle grip of his son's arm and marched him in triumph from the field.

"Between school hours and work, Jack found time to pore over books of history, poetry and fiction, and to nurse the secret wish to become a writer. He was graduated from the Oakland grammar school at fourteen, and a few months later drifted into an adventurous life 'long shore. Here he shared the industries and pastimes of the marine population huddled along the water-front, taking his chances at salmon fishing, oyster pirating, schooner sailing, and other bay-faring ventures, never holding himself aloof when comrades were awake, but when they slept turning to his book with the avidity of a mind athirst for knowledge."

Yet in spite of his general camaraderie he was a solitary youth. Speaking again of his mental and spiritual isolation from his fellows at this time, London said:

"I belonged to a 'street gang' in West Oakland, as rough and tough a crowd as you'll find in any city in the country. Yet while I always got along well with the crowd—I was sociable and held up my end when it came to doing anything—I was never in the center of things; I was always alone, in a corner, as it were.

"Then it was that I learned to hate the city. I suppose my father and mother looked upon it as childish prejudice, but I clearly saw the futility of life in such a herd. I was oppressed with a deadly oppression as I saw that all the people, rich and poor alike, were merely mad creatures, chasing phantoms. Now and again my inner thoughts were so intense that I could not keep them to myself. My sympathies and emotions were so aroused that I would talk out to a few of the gang that which surged, boiled and seethed within me. There was nothing of the preacher about me, but a spirit of rebellion against the hypnotism that had fallen upon the poor. They had it in their own hands to remedy the evils that beset them, yet they

were obsessed by the idea that their lot was God-ordained, fixed, immovable. How that cursed idea used to irritate me. How it fired my tongue. The boys would listen open mouthed and wide eyed, but few of them catching even a glimmer of the thoughts that were surging through me. Then men would be attracted to the little crowd of boys, hearing the tense, fierce voice assailing them. Thus, little by little, I was led on—urged at the same time by the voice within—to harangue the crowds on Oakland streets, and be-

came known as the Boy Socialist.

"Doubtless it was all crude and rude, illogical and inconsequential, but it was the most serious matter to me, and has had much to do with shaping my later thought and life. At the same time the hopelessness of arousing my own class so smote me, and the heartlessness of the moneyed class so wounded me that I begged and urged my father and mother to let me go to sea.

"Accordingly, when I was seventeen, in the fall of 1893, I was allowed to ship before the mast on a sailing schooner which cruised to Japan and up the North Coast to the Russian side of the Behring Sea. We touched at Yokohama, and I got my first seductive taste of the Orient. We stayed in Japan three weeks. While we were on the high seas the captain tried to pay the crew in foreign coin. We refused to take it, as there was a discount on it which meant considerable loss to us. He insisted. We rebelled, and for a time had a real mutiny on board, and if the captain hadn't finally given in, there's no knowing what might have happened to me, as I was just as forward in protesting as any of the others, though I was the youngest sailor aboard."

That Jack not only resented injustice from the captain, but from his messmates, the following incident, related by Mrs. Eames, clearly shows:

"Our sailor man one day sat on his bunk weaving a mat of rope yarn when he was gruffly accosted by a burly Swede taking his turn at 'peggy-day' (a fo'castle term, signifying a sailor's day for cleaning off the meals, washing up the dishes, and filling the slush-lamps), a part of which disagreeable tasks the man evidently hoped to bull-doze the green hand into doing for him.

" 'Here, you landlubber,' he bawled with an oath, 'fill up the molasses. You eat the most of it!'

"Jack, usually the most amiable of the hands, bristled at his roughness; besides, he had vivid memories of his first and only attempt to eat the black, viscous stuff booked 'molasses' on the fo'castle bill of fare, and so indignantly denied the charge.

" 'I never taste it. 'Tain't fit for a hog. It's your day to grub, so do it yourself.'

"Not a messmate within hearing of the altercation but pictured disaster to this beardless, undersized boy.

"Jack's defiant glance again dropped to his mat, and he quietly went on twisting the yarn. At this the sailor, both arms heaped with dishes, swore the harder, and threatened blood curd-

ling consequences if he were not obeyed, but Jack kept silent, his supple hands nimbly intent on the rope strands, though the tail of his eye took note of his enemy.

"Another threat, met by exasperating indifference, and the incensed Swede dropped the coffee pot to give a back handed slap on the boy's curled mouth. The instant after iron hard knuckles struck squarely between the sailor's eyes, followed by the crash of crockery. The Swede, choking with rage, made a lunge at Jack with a sledge-hammer fist, but the latter dodged, and like a flash vaulted to the ruffian's back, his fingers knitting in the fellow's throat-pipes. He bellowed and charged like a mad bull, and with every frenzied jump, Jack's head was a battering ram against the deck beams. Down crashed the slush lamp and the lookers-on drew up their feet in the bunks to make room for the show; they saw what the Swede did not—that Jack was getting the worst of it. His eyes bulged horribly and his face streamed blood, but he only dug his fingers deeper into that flesh-padded larynx and yelled through his shut teeth: 'Will you promise to let me alone? Eh—will you promise?'

"The Swede, tortured and purple in the face, gurgled an assent, and when that viselike grip on his throat loosened, reeled and stumbled to his knees like a felled bullock. The sailors, jamming their way through a wild clutter of food and broken dishes, crowded around the jubilant hero of the hour with friendly offers of assistance and a noticeable increase of respect in their tone and manner. Thence on Jack had his 'peggy-day' like the rest, his mates risking no further attempt to take advantage of his youth or inexperience."

On his return to California he felt, more than ever before, his need for study. He joined the "Henry Clay Debating Society," and entered into its work with a fierce zest that his companions were unable to understand. Reflection while doing solitary duties on the high seas had led him to see also that he had better seek to know

The author on horseback rounds over his extensive land holdings, Sonoma County, California.

the ideas of the leading men of thought. Surely somewhere he would find the explanation of the inconsistencies and inhumanities of life. As he himself says in his "What Life Means to Me.":

"I had been born in the working class, and I was now, at the age of eighteen, beneath the point at which I had started. I was down in the cellar of society, down in the subterranean depths of misery about which it is neither nice nor proper to speak. I was in the pit, the abyss, the human cesspool, the shambles and the charnel house of our civilization. This is the part of the edifice of society that society chooses to ignore. Lack of space compels me here to ignore it, and I shall say only that the things I there saw gave me a terrible scare.

"I was scared into thinking. I saw the naked simplicities of the compli-cated civilization in which I lived. Life was a matter of food and shelter. In order to get food and shelter men sold things. The merchant sold shoes, the politician sold his manhood, and the representative of the people, with exceptions, of course, sold his trust; while nearly all sold their honor. All things were commodities, all people bought and sold. The one commodity that labor had to sell was muscle. The honor of labor had no price in the market place. Labor had muscle and muscle alone, to sell.

"But there was a difference, a vital difference. Shoes and trust and honor had a way of renewing themselves. They were imperishable stocks. Muscle, on the other hand, did not renew. As the shoe merchant sold shoes, he continued to replenish his stock. But there was no way of replenishing the laborer's stock of muscle. The more he sold of his muscle the less of it remained to him. It was his one commodity, and each day his stock of it diminished. In the end, if he did not die before, he sold out and put up his shutters. He was a muscle bankrupt, and nothing remained to him but to go down into the cellar of society and perish miserably.

"I learned further that brain was likewise a commodity. It, too, was different from muscle. A brain seller was only at his prime when he was fifty or sixty years old, and his wares were fetching higher prices than ever. But a laborer was worked out or broken down at forty-five or fifty. I had been in the cellar of society, and I did not like the place as a habitation. The pipes and drains were unsanitary, and the air was bad to breathe. If I could not live on the parlor floor of society, I could, at any rate, have a try at the attic. It was true the diet there was slim, but the air at least was pure. So I resolved to sell no more muscle and to become a vender of brains.

"Then began a frantic pursuit of knowledge. While thus equipping myself to become a brain merchant, it was inevitable that I should delve into sociology. There I found, in a certain class of books, scientifically formulated, the simple sociological concepts I had already worked out for myself. Other and greater minds, before I was born, had worked out all that I had thought, and a vast deal more. I discovered that I was a Socialist."

He had long been a Socialist without knowing it, but now he was conscious of his real affiliations. This led him into a singular experience. The "Henry Clay" had planned for an open debate in which London was to take an important part. When the time arrived Jack was nowhere to be found. Coxey had left Oakland a few days before with his army of the unemployed. The sudden impulse had thereupon seized Jack to follow. The result of this experience has been told with graphic power by London in his "The Road." I suppose no book of his has been so severely criticised as this. It has been stated again and again that he took this trip for the purpose of making sociological studies. The fact is, he was a mere lad, worked to death, because he was forced to do the work of men to earn enough to keep the family going. He had no idea at the time of making an investigation or writing so far as "The Road" was concerned. Curiosity, adventure, freedom—all these, but study, as Professor Wyckoff did, never entered his imagination.

When he discovered his gift of writing, here, however, was a wonderful mine of personal material ready made to his hand. It had never before been handled as he could handle it. For the first time he exposes the innermost life of the tramp.

In effect he says: "This I was, and what I was the . . . hundreds of thousands of tramps and hoboes that daily walk this country *are*." His is no fancy picture. It is a stern setting forth of facts, and whether I approve of London's method of getting the facts or not, I have sense enough to perceive the importance of them to me and to every other decent and law abiding citizen. Here is this vast army of lying, thieving, prowling, festering manstuff. What are we doing, intelligently and wisely, to break it up and change its individual elements into useful citizenship? Personally I am grateful to London for giving me the inner facts, and I will not quarrel with his conscience if he is able to reconcile it with doing what he did *on my behalf*.

There is more, however, to the book than I have indicated. As a reviewer in the Los Angeles Times wrote:

"The book is valuable also in other ways. London is a powerful and virile writer, and he has both material and manner in the present case. The chapter telling how a tramp steals a ride on a railway train is as thrilling and breath-bating as a fragment from Dumas—it is a veritable novel of adventure put in a score of pages. London's record of his experiences in the penitentiary is another chapter, where the material of a report on prison condi-

Jack London inspecting one of the vineyards on his ranch, Valley of the Moon.

tions, a melodrama and a novel are condensed into a sharp, incisive short story, all done with fine literary skill."

That penitentiary experience is one that every American ought to read and ponder. We pride ourselves on our Constitution and our deference to law. London shows that the tramp has no rights according to the Constitution, and that the law is ruthlessly trampled upon by men who are sworn to uphold it. He was arrested, thrust into prison, brought before a magistrate, refused his inherent right to plead guilty or not guilty, compelled by threats of severer punishment to keep silent while he was being sentenced contrary to law, and then illegally, by brute force, exactly as if he were in Russia and being sent to the mines of Siberia, was marched to the State penitentiary and compelled to serve out his sentence.

Personally I have no hesitation in saying that the Court which so sentenced him and the officers who knowingly carried out the sentence are more dangerous to this country and subver-

sive of its high ideals than all the tramps and hoboes that can be found in a day's journey.

To London, however, this was but one more experience, adding to his store of knowledge and giving more grist for the literary mill that he felt sure at some time soon would be set in motion. He returned to California mainly on the brake-beam route of the Canadian Pacific. Arrived here, he plunged into securing an education with his characteristic energy and determination. But his tramp experiences had not lessened his zeal on behalf of "his class." More than ever he resolved to help ameliorate their hard condition. Like William Morris, and fired with the same passion for humanity, he placed himself at the disposal of the Socialist Labor Party, and they sent him here and there to speak on their behalf. Fearless and bold to the last degree, he refused to obey the policeman set to enforce a newly passed ordinance prohibiting public speaking on the streets. He was arrested. But when the case came to trial he defended himself with such dignity and logic that he was immediately acquitted.

This, however, was only a part of his life. His deepest need and cry now was for an education. And how earnest he was to secure it. For awhile he attended the high school in Oakland; then, to hurry up matters, took a three months' course at Anderson's Academy.· But the private school was both too tedious and too expensive, so he determined to prepare himself for the university by private study. In "Martin Eden" he thus tells of his reply when urged to go to a night school.

"It seems so babyish for me to be going to night school. But I wouldn't mind that if I thought it would pay. But I don't think it will pay. I can do the work quicker than they can teach me. It would be a loss of time, etc. . . . I have a feeling that I am a natural student. I can study by myself. I take to it kindly, like a duck to water. You see yourself what I did with grammar. And I've learned much of other things—you would never dream how much."

With all his preparation for the University, the pressure of life and its needs was so great that he was able only to attend during his freshman year. It was during this time that he began to attend socialistic meetings in San Francisco and came in personal contact with some of the leaders. In "What Life Means to Me" he tells of his experiences: "Here I found keen-flashing intellects and brilliant wits; for here I met strong and alert-brained, withal horny-handed members of the working class; unfrocked preachers too wide in their Christianity for any congregation of Mammon worshipers; professors broken in the wheel of university subservience to the ruling class and flung out because they were quick with knowledge which they strove to apply to the affairs of mankind.

"Here I found also warm faith in the human, glowing idealism, sweetness of unselfishness, renunciation and martyrdom—all the splendid, stinging things of the spirit. Here life was clean, noble and alive. Here, life rehabilitated itself, became wonderful and glorious; and I was glad to be alive. I was in touch with great souls who exalted flesh and spirit over dollars and cents; and to whom the thin wail of the starved slum child meant more than all the pomp and circumstance of commercial expansion and world-empire. All about me were nobleness of purpose and heroism of effort, and all my days and nights were sunshine and starshine, all fire and dew, with before my eyes, ever burning and blazing, the Holy Grail, Christ's own Grail, the warm human, long-suffering and maltreated, but to be rescued and saved at the last."

* * * *

In "Martin Eden" he tells us somewhat more in detail one of his first meetings with the Socialist leaders. The "Brissenden" of "Martin Eden" is based upon George Sterling, the poet, who in those days was warmly stirred with earnest desire to help improve the condition of his fellow-men. With him he visited some of the leaders in San Francisco. Here is part of London's description of that meeting:

"At first the conversation was desultory. Nevertheless, Martin could not fail to appreciate the keen play of their minds. They were men with opinions, though the opinions often clashed, and, though they were witty and clever, they were not superficial. He swiftly saw, no matter upon what they talked, that each man applied the correlation of knowledge and had also a deep-seated and unified conception of society and the Cosmos. Nobody manufactured their opinions for them; they were all rebels of one variety or another, and their lips were strangers to platitudes. Never had Martin, at the Morses', heard so amazing a range of topics discussed. There seemed no limit save time to the things they were alive to. The talk wandered from Mrs. Humphrey Ward's new book to Shaw's latest play, through the future of the drama to reminiscences of Mansfield. They appreciated or sneered at the

The half finished patio of "Wolf House" before the ruinous fire.

morning editorials, jumped from labor conditions in New Zealand, to Henry James and Brander Matthews, passed on to the German designs in the Far East and the economic aspects of the Yellow Peril, wrangled over the German elections and Bebel's last speech, and settled down to local politics, the latest plans and scandals in the union labor party administration, and the wires that were pulled to bring about the Coast Seamen's strike. Martin was struck by the inside knowledge they possessed. They knew what was never printed in the newspapers—the wires and strings and the hidden hands that made the puppets dance. To Martin's surprise, the girl, Mary, joined in the conversation, displaying an intelligence he had never encountered in the few women he had met. They talked together on Swinburn and Rosetti, after which she led him beyond his depths into the by-paths of French literature. His revenge came when she defended Maeterlinck, and he brought into action the carefully thought out thesis of 'The Shame of the Sun.'

"Several other men had dropped in, and the air was thick with tobacco smoke, when Brissenden waved the red flag.

"'Here's fresh meat for your axe, Kreis,' he said, 'a rose white youth with the ardor of a lover for Herbert Spencer. Make a Haeckelite of him—if you can.'

"Kreis seemed to wake up and flash like some metallic, magnetic thing, while Norton looked at Martin sympathetically, with a sweet, girlish smile, as much as to say that he would be amply protected.

"Kreis began directly on Martin, but step by step Norton interfered, until he and Kreis were off and away in a personal battle. Martin listened and fain would have rubbed his eyes. It was impossible that this should be, much less in the labor ghetto south of Market. The books were alive in these men. They talked with fire and enthusiasm, the intellectual stimulant stirring them as he had seen drink and anger stir other men. What he heard was no longer the philosophy of the dry, printed word, written by half-mythical demigods like Kant and Spencer. It was living philosophy, with warm, red blood, incarnated in these two men till its very features worked with excitement. Now and again other men joined in, and all followed the discussion with cigarettes going out in their hands, and with alert, intent faces.

"Idealism had never attracted Martin, but the exposition it now received at the hands of Norton was a revelation. The logical plausibility of it, that made an appeal to his intellect, seemed missed by Kreis and Hamilton, who sneered at Norton as a metaphysician, and who, in turn, sneered back at them at metaphysicians. *Phenomenon* and *noumenon* were bandied back and forth. They charged him with attempting to explain consciousness by itself. He charged them with word-jugglery, with reasoning from words to theory instead of from facts to theory. At this they were aghast. It was the cardinal tenet of their mode of reasoning to start with the facts and to give names to the facts.

"When Norton wandered into the intricacies of Kant, Kreis reminded him that all good little German philosophies when they died went to Oxford. A little later Norton reminded them of Hamilton's Law of Parsimony, the application of which they immediately claimed for every reasoning process of theirs. And Martin hugged his knees and exulted in it all. But Norton was no Spencerian, and he, too, strove for Martin's philosophic soul, talking as much at him as to his two opponents.

" 'You know Berkeley has never been answered,' he said, looking directly at Martin. 'Herbert Spencer came the nearest, which was not very near. Even the staunchest of Spencer's followers will not go farther. I was reading an essay of Saleeby's the other day, and the best Saleeby could say was that Herbert Spencer *nearly* succeeded in answering Berkeley.'

" 'You know what Hume said?' Hamilton asked. Norton nodded, but Hamilton gave it for the benefit of the rest. 'He said that Berkeley's arguments admit of no answer and produce no conviction.'

" 'In his, Hume's mind,' was the reply. 'And Hume's mind was the same as yours, with this difference: he was wise enough to admit there was no answering Berkeley.'

"Norton was sensitive and excitable though he never lost his head, while Kreis and Hamilton were like a pair of cold-blooded savages, seeking out tender places to prod and poke. As the evening grew late, Norton, smarting under the repeated charges of being a metaphysician, clutching his chair to keep from jumping to his feet, his gray eyes snapping and his girlish face grown harsh and sure, made a grand attack upon their position.

" 'All right, you Haeckelites, I may reason like a medicine man, but, pray, how do you reason? You have nothing to stand on, you unscientific dogmatists, with your positive science which you are always lugging about into places it has no right to be. Long before the school of materialistic monism arose, the ground was removed so there could be no foundation. Locke was the man, John Locke. Two hundred years ago—more than that, even —in his "Essay concerning the Human Understanding,' he proved the non-existence of innate ideas. The best of it is that that is precisely what you claim. To-night, again and again, you have asserted the non-existence of innate ideas.'

" 'And what does that mean? It means that you can never know ultimate reality. Your brains are empty when you are born. Appearances, or phenomena, are all the content your minds can receive from your five senses. Then noumena, which are not in your minds when you are born, have no way of getting in——'

" 'I deny——' Kreis started to interrupt.

" 'You wait till I'm done,' Norton shouted. 'You can know only that much of the play and interplay of force and matter as impinges in one way or another on your senses. You see, I am willing to admit, for the sake of the argument, that matter exists;

"Wolf House" before the destructive fire.

and what I am about to do is to efface you by your own argument. I can't do it any other way, for you are both congenitally unable to understand a philosophic abstraction.

" 'And now, what do you know of matter, according to your own positive science? You know it is only by its phenomena, its appearances. You are aware only of its changes, or of such changes in it as cause changes in your consciousness. Positive science deals only with phenomena, yet you are foolish enough to strive to be ontologists and to deal with noumena. Yet, by the very definition of positive science, science is concerned only with appearances. As somebody has said, phenomenal knowledge cannot transcend phenomena.

" 'You cannot answer Berkeley, even if you have annihilated Kant, and yet, perforce, you assume that Berkeley is wrong when you affirm that science proves the non-existence of God, or, as much to the point, the existence of matter. You know I granted the reality of matter only in order to make myself intelligible to your understanding. Be positive scientists, if you

please, but ontology has no place in positive science, so leave it alone. Spencer is right in his agnosticism, but if Spencer——'

"But it was time to catch the last ferry boat to Oakland, and Brissenden and Martin slipped out, leaving Norton still talking and Kreis and Hamilton waiting to pounce on him like a pair of hounds as soon as he finished.

" 'You have given me a glimpse of fairyland,' Martin said on the ferry boat. 'It makes life worth while to meet people like that. My mind is all worked up. I never appreciated idealism before. Yet I can't accept it. I know that I shall always be a realist. I am made so, I guess. But I'd like to have made a reply to Kreis and Hamilton, and I think I'd have had a word or two for Norton. I didn't see that Spencer was damaged any. I'm as excited as a child on its first visit to the circus. I see I must read up some more. I'm going to get hold of Saleeby. I still think Spencer is unassailable, and next time I'm going to take a hand myself.'

"But Brissenden, breathing painfully, had dropped off to sleep, his

The ruins of the "House that Jack Built." Three years were spent in the keen enjoyment of its planning and construction. Fire destroyed it, 1913.

chin buried in a scarf and resting on his sunken chest, his body wrapped in the long overcoat and shaking to the vibration of the propellers."

While still at the University the Klondike gold excitement struck San Francisco. London was one of the first to yield to the lure. As Mrs. Payne writes: "He was among the few doughty argonauts who at this season made it over the Chilcoot Pass, the great majority waiting for spring. As charges were forty-three cents per pound for carrying supplies a distance of thirty miles, from salt water to fresh, he packed his thousand pound outfit, holding his own with the strongest and most experienced in the party.

"And here in this still white world of the North, where nature makes the most of every vital throb that resists her cold, and man learns the awful significance and emphasis of Arctic life and action, young London came consciously into his heritage. He would write of these—the terrorizing of an Alaskan landscape, its great peaks bulging with century-piled snows, its woods rigid, tense and

voiced by the frost like strained cat-gut; the fierce howls of starving wolf-dogs; the tracks of the dog-teams marking the lonely trail; but more than all else, the human at the North Pole.

"Thus it would seem that his actual development as a writer began on the trail, though at the time he set no word to paper, not even jottings by the way in a note-book. A tireless brooding on the wish to write shaped his impulse to definite purpose, but outwardly he continued to share the interests and labors of his companion prospectors.

"After a year spent in that weirdly picturesque but hazardous life, he succumbed to scurvy, and, impatient of the delay of homebound steamers, he and two camp-mates decided to embark in an open boat for the Behring Sea. The three accordingly made the start midway in June, and the voyage turned out to be a memorably novel and perilous one—nineteen hundred miles of river in nineteen days!"

*   *   *   *

It was on his return from the Klondike that he found himself as a literary artist. He wrote an Alaskan story entitled "The Man on Trail," and sent it to the Overland Monthly. Its vivid and picturesque realism won it immediate acceptance, and soon thereafter the author, "a young man, plainly dressed, of modest and even boyish appearance," entered the editor's sanctum with a second story, "The White Silence."

In less than six months his fame was made. As he says in "What Life Means to Me": "As a brain-merchant I was a success. Society opened its portals to me. I entered right in on the parlor floor. I sat down to dinner with the masters of society and with the wives and daughters of the masters of society. The women were gowned beautifully, I admit; but to my naive surprise I discovered that they were of the same clay as all the rest of the women I had known down below in the cellar. 'The colonel's lady and Judy O'Grady were sisters under their skins'—and gowns."

From that day to this, his power and popularity have never waned. Granted that some books and stories are less powerful than others—that is merely to acknowledge that he is human and is not always at the supreme height of invention and creation. But certainly his last volume of South Sea stories, published under the title "A Son of the Sun," shows no diminution of power either in observation, reflection or word picturing.

In appearance, London is a broad-shouldered fellow, with small hands and feet, standing five feet eight inches high, weighing one hundred and eighty pounds stripped, with a flexible mouth over a strong, resolute chin. He has the look of an athlete, and his shoulders and aggressive movements clearly suggest that he is prepared physically to force his way through the crowd, taking his share of the jostle and giving as good as, or better, than he takes. While not defiant of his fellows, he quietly enjoys the comments sometimes made on his appearance. On one occasion I stood by him and we distinctly heard a

passerby exclaim: "That's Jack London. He looks like a prize-fighter, doesn't he?" Jack looked at me and winked a clear wink of appreciation of the honor thus conferred upon him. In the copy of "The Game," which he described and sent to me, he wrote: "I'd rather be champion of the world than President of the United States." One of his proud moments was when, in Quito, Ecuador, he was mistaken by a group of small Spaniards for a bull-fighter.

He believes fully in keeping his physical frame in order. He is essentially a physical culturist. He swims, rows, canoes, fences, boxes, swings a sledge, throws a hammer, runs and rides horseback fifty miles a day if necessary. A year ago I called on him when he had just returned from a three months' driving trip, where he tooled a coach, with four-in-hand, over the steep and rough mountainous roads of California and Oregon. Baring his arm he bade me feel his muscles—biceps and lower arm—as he relaxed and then tightened them. They were like living steel.

He sleeps in an open-air porch with lights, books and writing material always at hand. Directly he awakens he begins either to read or make notes, always using a pencil for his writing. When breakfast time comes, if he has any intimate friends as guests whom he cares to meet, he rises and eats and chats with them for half an hour or so. His breakfasts are very simple. After breakfast he retires to his library, and nothing is allowed to disturb him until he has completed his daily "stint." This is never less than one thousand words, and he generally keeps at it until noon, making his work as perfect as possible and outlining what he will undertake on the following day. He never rewrites. In all my many visits to him I have never known him to deviate from his regular routine but once, and that was on the occasion of the visit of my Boston friend.

Many people, like myself, have wondered where he obtains all his in-

Another view of "Wolf House" ruins.

finite variety of plots for his short stories and novels. Month after month, year after year, he pours forth his stream of short stories, all of them good, though some are better than others. Not one, however, fails in human interest; it may not please you, but it grips you, fascinates you, compels you. For it is human, powerful and full of a robust life.

Where does he get the germ of these stories? Where do they come from? Are they pure pieces of fiction, or cleverly disguised stories of fact? If the former, one wonders at the fecundity of his brain; it becomes one of the marvels of genius; if the latter, one wonders equally at the marvelous genius of his observation.

That his imagination is a fertile and brilliant one there can be no question, and undoubtedly such a virile and creative mind as his finds far less difficulty in the construction of plots than most writers do. But here is an illustration which he himself gave to me, of his methods of taking a dramatic episode that had come to his attention and weaving an apparently entirely different story from it. We were talking upon this subject, and he took down from his book shelf "Wigwam and War Path," by A. B. Meacham. Mr. Meacham was superintendent of Indian affairs and chairman of the Modoc Peace Commission of which General Canby and Dr. Thomas were also members. It will be remembered that the Modoc Indians of the Klamath region in Southern Oregon and Northern California had long been insolent and on the war path. Meacham shows that their insolence and hostility were gendered by the wicked, cruel and murderous conduct of unprincipled white men. There had been several conflicts between the whites and the Indians, and finally it was decided to appoint a Peace Commission. One of Meacham's good friends was Frank Riddle, who, having married a Modoc wife, who was known as Tobey, was allowed to sit in council with the Indians. Tobey, though an Indian, was a woman of natural refinement, high integrity and deep devotion. She was loyalty itself. Having bestowed her friendship upon Mr. Meacham nothing could prevail upon her to betray him. Consequently when she learned that the leaders of the Modocs contemplated the treacherous murder of the members of the Peace Commission, she stealthily went by night and gave warning to Mr. Meacham, though she was well aware that by this act she signed her own death warrant. For she knew the Indians would reason the matter out, and, if their plans were foiled, would know that some one had betrayed them, and that she was the only one who would be guilty of treachery to her own race. "Now," said Mr. London, "look at that woman. She was loyal to Mr. Meacham in spite of the fact that he was hated by her people. He was a representative of the whites who in every way had injured her own tribe. Yet she gave him a devotion that she knew would certainly bring a vindictive death upon herself.

"I intend to use that woman as the main character of a strong story. I do not know where I will place her, but in the South Seas, in the frozen North, in the sunny South, in Australia, somewhere, somehow, I am going to use that woman."

In "Martin Eden" he sets this idea before his reader in his own way, as follows:

"Martin began, that morning, a story which he had sketched out a number of weeks before and which ever since had been worrying him with its insistent clamor to be created.

"Apparently it was to be a rattling sea story, a tale of twentieth century adventure and romance, handling real characters, in a real world, under real conditions. But beneath the swing and go of the story was to be something else—something that the superficial reader would never discern, and which, on the other hand, would not diminish in any way the interest and enjoyment for such a reader. It was this, and not the mere story, that impelled Martin to write it. For that matter, it was always the great, universal motif that suggested plots to him. After having found such a motif, he cast about for the particular persons and particular location in time and space wherewith and wherein to utter the universal thing."

*   *   *   *

While London is essentially and primarily an artist in his literary work, he is also a profound philosopher and humanitarian. Hence everything he writes has a distinct purpose. That purpose may not always be apparent to the careless and casual observer, but it is there, all the same. I doubt if he ever wrote a single thing in which some philosophy is not clearly taught or some humanizing influence deliberately interwoven. "The Call of the Wild" is a clear lesson in "reversion to type," for London is a firm believer in the doctrine of evolution. At least he accepts it as the best workable theory at present advanced by the scientists to account for the upward and onreaching tendencies of mankind. On the other hand "White Fang" is a marvelous story of the controlling and modifying influences—the civilizing and uplifting power—of love and tenderness, of the real spirit of humanity. "Burning Daylight" contains a dozen lessons. It shows how any great minded man can become a "master of finances" if he wishes to so limit himself, and then, with graphic power, it shows how such a one gradually becomes absorbed in his business until he is a mere money-getting machine. The fact that the hero, in spite of his millions, could not win his typewriter to marry him, is London's defense of the "workers" against a too-sweeping charge of money-hunger or unworthy cupidity, while his hero's return to sanity (as he regards it) comes when he deliberately throws away his wealth—that which has demoralized him and keeps him from winning the woman of his affections—and retires, a poor man, to the simple life of a rancher in the beautiful Sonoma Valley.

"Before Adam" is a scientific treatise in popular form on pre-Adamic evolution, and "Martin Eden" is a studied incitement to the highest achievement.

His various "Social Studies" are important philosophical and sociological presentments, set forth with a soul asurge and a brain afire with the rights of the common man. However much we may differ from London we cannot deny the fiery power, the tremendous forcefulness of what he says, and the graphic intensity of his convictions.

"The Iron Heel" is a lesson and a warning, based upon historic studies, and he is a short-sighted reader of the analyses of the causes of the decline of other nations who pooh-poohs the solemn and portentous prophecies of this book. The imaginary horrors depicted are to be averted only by changing our mental attitude toward certain of the social and economic problems of the day.

* * * *

All his short stories have also a fine purpose. Take his story of "The Nature Man." How full it is of the healthful and curative powers of pure air, pure, fresh vegetable and fruit food, the sunlight and a natural life. All the Naturopaths combined never wrote as strong a plea for their theories as this story presents.

In speaking with London one day about this phase of his work he exclaimed: "Certainly! I no more believe in the 'art for art's sake' theory than I believe that a human and humane motive justifies an inartistic telling of a story. I believe there are saints in slime as well as saints in heaven, and it depends how the slime saints are treated—upon their environment—as to whether they will ever leave the slime or not. People find fault with me for my 'disgusting realism.' Life is full of disgusting realism. I know men and women as they are—millions of them yet in the slime stage. But I am an evolutionist, therefore a broad optimist, hence my love for the human (in the slime though he be) comes from my knowing him as he is and seeing the divine possibilities ahead of him. That's the whole motive of my 'White Fang.' Every atom of organic life is plastic. The finest specimens now in existence were once all pulpy infants capable of being moulded this way or that. Let the pressure be one way and we have atavism—the reversion to the wild; the other the domestication, civilization. I have always been impressed with the awful plasticity of life, and I feel that I can never lay enough stress upon the marvelous power and influence of environment."

In spite, therefore, of the superficial criticisms London's work has encountered, I venture the prediction that this feature will more and more receive recognition, until he will be regarded not only as a master writer of fiction, but as a keen philosopher, ruggedly, but none the less earnestly, bent on helping upward and forward his fellow-men.

I suppose after "The Call of the Wild," "Martin Eden" is one of the most popular of London's books. This was originally published in the Pacific Monthly, a western magazine formerly published at Portland, but now absorbed by the Sunset at San Francisco.

The manuscript of this novel had rather an interesting history. London had had some dispute with the former editor of the Pacific Monthly, and he had vowed that they should never have anything more from his pen. Soon after his departure on the "Snark" voyage, his business agent happening to meet a representative of the Pacific Monthly in San Francisco, told him what a great story "Martin Eden" was and suggested that it would make a first class serial which he could use for pushing up the circulation of his magazine. He asked the price and rather gasped when told that the serial rights would cost $9,000. He then asked how much a week's option would cost. "Five hundred dollars," was the reply. He signed a check for this amount and took the manuscript. Before the end of the week he met the agent in San Francisco and paid the $9,000 for the story. It certainly made a great impression and was doubtless well worth the amount.

The unconventionality, the simplicity, the daring and the absolute audacity of Jack London, which in an academically trained man might be considered unpardonable and appalling egotism, is best illustrated in this wonderful book of veiled biography. Where else before has a man so dared to reveal himself before the world?

This photograph was taken the day Mrs. London first met Jack London (1900.) It was taken to illustrate a story he was at that time writing for Overland Monthly, the first magazine to recognize his genius and to publish his stories. The six stories of the first series were colored with his then recent experiences in Alaska.

Even Rousseau in his "Confessions," Jean Paul Richter in his varied books upon himself, Goethe in "Wilhelm," never so freely, so fully, so explicitly analyzed themselves, their ambitions, motives and inner characters as has Jack London in "Martin Eden." And it is more in the concluding chapters, where, with an artistry that is perfect in its illusion of simplicity and naivete he analyzes his successes and the effect they have upon the world at large, upon editors and publishers, upon his loving but ignorant sister and her irretrievably vulgar and commercial husband, upon the father and mother of the girl he loved, and finally upon her (all fictitious characters, of

3

course) that he reveals the independence of his genius, the solitariness of his methods and the influence of this shut-off Western World upon his soul.

*   *   *   *

Let me here interject a few words to those literary aspirants who are finding difficulty in getting their efforts accepted by editors, and who imagine that Jack London leaped instantly into fame at his first endeavors. There never was a greater mistake made than this supposition. For years prior to the success of his Alaska stories he had been bombarding the magazines, just as he relates the story in "Martin Eden." First he tried poetry, but it all came back. He varied the forms, tried everything from couplets and limericks to sonnets and blank verse, but all were equally ineffective. Then he wrote plays, two-act, three-act, and four-act, but they had no better success. Then he tried the "society stunt," both in prose and verse, but he failed to catch the proper swing. Next he wrote Emersonian essays, and thundering philippics after Carlyle, occasionally varying his efforts with historic sketches and descriptions. But all alike failed, and a less resolute being would have been utterly and completely discouraged. This made his triumph all the more wonderful when it did come, especially as he seemed to leap into fame at a single bound.

London is most systematic in his method of work. "He devotes himself to his labors with care and precision, coining his time with miserly stint and observng a method of collecting and classification as amusing as it is effective. Across an angle of his study he stretches what he calls his 'clothes line,' a wire on which are strung batches of excerpts and notes fastened on by clothes' pins, the kind with a wire spring. A hastily scribbled thought and an extract bearing upon the same theme are duly clamped in their proper place, and the 'clothes line' usually dangles a dozen or more of these bunched tatters of literature. "His plan of reading has also a like

simplicity, with a hazard at economy of vital force. He does not read books consecutively, but collectively. A dozen volumes are selected on divers subjects—science, philosophy, fiction, et cetera, and arranged with regard to their relative profundity. Then he begins with the weightiest matter, reads it until his brain is a trifle wearied, when he lays the work aside for one requiring less effort, and so on all down the graded list, until at one sitting he has delved into each, always bringing up finally with the novel or poetry as the wine and walnuts of his literary feast."

London has been fiercely criticized and assailed for his intense and vivid pictures of the primitive, the rude, the savage, the uncontrolled in man. Some have said he has wildly exaggerated, others that nothing is gained by making such record, even if true. I take issue with both kinds of critics. It is impossible to exaggerate what man has done and the how of its doing. No man's imagination can go beyond what man has actually done. As London himself says in his "Burning Daylight," after describing a Klondike carouse on his hero's birthday: "Men have so behaved since the world began, feasting, fighting and carousing, whether in the dark cave mouth or by the fire of the squatting place, in the palaces of imperial Rome and the rock strongholds of robber barons, or in the sky-aspiring hotels of modern times and in the boozing dens of sailortown."

It was not until I read London's stories on the Alaska Indians that my entire heart warmed thoroughly toward him. For thirty years I have studied the Indians of the Southwest, and by intimate association I have come to know them and love them. I have always resented what to me was a wicked and cruel attitude of certain Americans who declare "the only good Indian is a dead Indian." I have learned to appreciate their true worth, and to know the beauty and grandeur of their character when rightly understood. As I read London's stories under the general title of "Children of the Frost," I saw that he had gained the same opinion of the Indians that I had. He had penetrated below the rude exterior to the manhood within, and I have no hesitancy whatever in stating my belief that as a true interpreter of the Indian, Jack London deserves to rank with Fenimore Cooper, Major J. W. Powell, Lieutenant F. H. Cushing, Dr. J. W. Fewks, and Frederick W. Starr, whom I regard as the greatest ethnologists America has yet produced.

In one of our conversations the question arose as to which of his stories I liked best. I immediately turned the question upon him and asked: "Which do you like best?" He laughingly replied: "Guess." I replied: "I venture to assert that I can not only guess accurately, but that my judgment will be different from that of any critic who has yet ventured such an opinion upon your work." Then picking up this book, I opened to the last story in it, entitled: "The League of the Old Men," and exclaimed: "There is your best story. In it you have expressed the cry of an expiring people, and I know you could not have written it had you not felt it to the very depths."

Tears sprang into his eyes, and reaching out his hand, he gave me a warm handclasp and said: "You are right. Yet fewer people have seemed to appreciate that story than any story I have written, and my publishers report that a less number of that volume have been sold than any other of my books."

*   *   *

London, like Joaquin Miller, was the victim of much and persistent misrepresentation. He is an avowed Socialist. Many newspapers do not like Socialists, and they seize every possible opportunity to spread unpleasant news about those who are known to profess that faith. Sometimes they are not very particular as to whether their assertions are true or not. In speaking of this several times, and then giving my personal impressions of London,

people have said to me: "Why do you not make these things known?"

In order to help make them known, let me tell an experience I had a few months ago with a distinguished and well known Eastern writer and playwright. He had been an editorial writer on one of the foremost Boston dailies of high standing, was a university man of high ideals and academic standards, who a year or so before had become transplanted to the Pacific Coast and was then doing special editorial writing on one of the San Francisco papers. We dined together several times, and on one occasion the name of London came up. Naturally, I spoke of the things in London that pleased and interested me. To my amazement, my Boston friend opened up with a tirade, denouncing London from every possible standpoint. There was nothing good about him in any way.

Seeing that he was rabid, I decided to let him have his talk out and then quietly informed him that his tirade was nothing but a mass of prejudice, for, said I, "I refuse to accept this unjust and untruthful tirade as your judgment. Judgments imply knowledge. You have no knowledge, but simply a mass of erroneous beliefs gained from mendacious newspapers and other unreliable sources."

I happened to be planning to go up to Sacramento to see the Governor and thence to London's home at Glen Ellen the following day, and asked my editorial friend if he would not like to meet me and accompany me to see London and his wife. In his finest Bostonese he exclaimed: "But, my dear fellow, I have received no invitation."

Heartily laughing, I replied: "I have given you an invitation!"

"But," said he, "what about Mr. and Mrs. London?"

Again I laughed and said: "Let your New England conscience be perfectly at rest. I have invited you, and that is enough. You ought to know enough of me already to be sure that I should not invite you to any place where you would not be welcome."

"That being the case," said he, "nothing will give me greater pleasure. I shall love to study him at first hand, and after your severe criticism upon my 'prejudice,' I am more anxious than ever to see Mr. London and find out what I think of him after close personal contact."

According to arrangement we met the next evening. On our arrival at Glen Ellen we found the cart waiting for us, and after a delightful drive through the cool twilight we entered the spacious yard, where gigantic live-oaks of a thousand years' growth, bid one enter and rest. When we entered the large, long room of the old ranch house, now used by the Londons until their new home is finished, we found Mrs. London seated at the Steinway grand piano immediately on our left, and Jack with outstretched hands and cheery voice bidding us welcome. This was the first surprise my friend experienced. Our simple and hearty meal—served specially, as we had come upon a late evening train—shook him up a little more. It happened to be Hallowe'en—a fact I had forgotten, but Jack and his wife and other guests were most wide awake to it, for they had announced that fun was to be free and fast that night. The other guests were a friend of Mrs. London's—the sister of one of California's proudest artists—a young architect of San Francisco, and a Socialist comrade of Jack's, who had just happened in as he was tramping across the country. These, with Jack and his wife, my editorial friend and myself, made the party total up to seven, with the Japanese helper, Nakata, now and again assisting in making eight. I was in the mood for fun, so we plunged in. First, we hung up apples from a point above and sought to make bites in them without touching the "bobbing and dodging things" with our hands. Then a large plate of white flour was brought, the flour mounded up about five inches high, and in the center on the top of it was placed a dime. The seven of us now commenced a march around the table, each taking up a table knife as we approached the plate and cutting off a greater or less mass of the flour as we willed. At first this was easy, but as we cut nearer to the center it became a more delicate and risky task. For the game consisted in continuing to cut until the dime rested on the merest pedestal of flour, ready to crumble at a touch, and whoever gave that final touch was then required to place his hands behind his back and fish out the dime from the flour *with his teeth*. It was also freely stipulated beforehand that there should be no "dodging" and wiping off of the flour from the face until the victor stood alone with unfloured face. The hope and expectation, of course, was that I, with moustache and full beard of black should fall an early victim, but somehow the Fates favored me. First the "Comrade" guest failed, then Mr. London, then the woman guest, then my editorial friend— and it must be confessed that his cheeks and closely trimmed sandy moustache and wisp of beard, even his eyelashes, did look excruciatingly funny all whitened up with flour in dabs and patches—then the architect and finally Mrs. London, leaving me the proud and unfloured victor.

This only paved the way for another game and greater fun. We all laughed until our sides ached, and when finally we retired it was way into the "wee, sma' hours."

Now, as I have elsewhere explained, as it is London's custom to stick rigidly to his work in the morning, my editorial friend and I would have been left to our own devices until after lunch, but, just before we went to bed I said to Jack: "Why not take a holiday to-morrow, and instead of waiting till afternoon for our horseback ride, let's all go out together in the morning." Somewhat to my surprise he consented, and the horses were duly ordered. No sooner was breakfast over than we were off—the whole party of us. And what a ride it was! Let me give you here a part of London't own description of his ranch on which this wonderful ride took place.

"We let down the bars and crossed an upland meadow. Next we went over a low, oak covered ridge and descended into a smaller meadow Again we climbed a ridge, this time riding under red-limbed madronos and manzanitas of deeper red. The first rays of the sun streamed upon our backs as we climbed. A flight of quail thrummed off through the thickets. A big jack-rabbit crossed our path, leaping swiftly and silently like a deer. And then a deer, a many pronged buck, the sun flashing red-gold from neck and shoulders, cleared the crest of the ridge before us and was gone.

"We followed in his wake a space, then dropped down a zigzag trail that he disdained into a group of noble redwoods that stood about a pool of water murky with mineral from the mountain side. I knew every inch of the way. Once a writer friend of mine had owned the ranch; but he, too, had become a revolutionist, though more disastrously than I, for he was already dead and gone, and none knew where nor how. He alone, in the days he had lived, knew the secret of the hiding place for which I was bound. He had bought the ranch for beauty and paid a round price for it, much to the disgust of the local farmers. He used to tell with great glee how they were wont to shake their heads mournfully at the price, to accomplish ponderously a bit of mental arithmetic, and then to say: 'But you can't make six per cent on it.'

"Out of it he had made a magnificent deer park, where, over thousands of acres of sweet slopes and glades and canyons, the deer ran almost in primitive wilderness."

There are many springs, and these unite to make a stream which ever flows.

"A glade of tangled vines and bushes ran between two wooded knolls. The glade ended abruptly at the steep bank of a stream. It was a little stream, rising from springs, and the hottest summer never dried it up. On every hand were tall wooded knolls, a group of them, with all the seeming of having been flung there from some careless Titan's hand. There was no bed-rock in them. They rose from their bases hundreds of feet, and they were composed of red volcanic earth, the famous wine-soil of Sonoma. Through these the tiny stream had cut its deep and precipitous channel."

The arrangement for the purchase of part of the estate was made while London was away on the "Snark" trip. A crafty and cunning seller practically deceived Jack's agent by allowing to be inserted in the lease a clause entitling the owners of a brickyard nearby to excavate certain clays from a part of the ranch, which they needed for their business. But as they had to pay for it at a good price and soon found it the only profitable part of their business, Jack made a good thing out of it, so did not complain.

"This brickyard was close at hand," so he writes in "Burning Daylight, "on the flat beside the Sonoma Creek. The kilns were visible among the trees, when he glanced to the left and caught sight of wooded knolls half a mile away, perched on the rolling slopes of Sonoma Mountain. The mountain, itself wooded, towered behind. The trees on the knoll seemed to beckon to him. The dry, early summer air, shot through with sunshine, was wine to him. Unconsciously he drank it in in deep breaths. The prospect of the brickyard was uninviting. He was jaded with all things business, and the wooded knolls were calling to him. A horse between his legs—a good horse, he decided; one that sent him back to the cayuses he had ridden during his eastern Oregon boyhood. He had been somewhat of a rider in those early days, and the champ of bit and creak of saddle-leather sounded good to him now.

"Resolving to have his fun first and to look over the brickyard afterward, he rode up the hill, prospecting for a way across country to get to the knolls. He left the country road at the first gate he came to and cantered through a hayfield. The grain was waist-high on either side the wagon road, and he sniffed the warm aroma of it with delighted nostrils. Larks flew up before him, and from everywhere came mellow notes. From the appearance of the road it was patent that it had been used for hauling clay to the now idle brickyard. Salving his conscience with the idea that this was part of the inspection, he rode on to the clay pit—a huge scar in a hillside. But he did not linger long, swinging off again to the left and leaving the road. Not a farmhouse was in sight, and the change from the city crowding was essentially satisfying. He rode now through open woods, across little flower-scattered glades, till he came upon a spring. Flat on the ground, he drank deeply of the clear water, and, looking about him, felt with a shock the beauty of the world. It came to him like a discovery; he had never realized it before, he concluded, and also, he had forgotten much. One could not sit in at high finance and keep track of such things. As he drank in the air, the scene, and the distant song of larks, he felt like a poker player rising from a night long table and coming forth from the pent atmosphere to taste the freshness of the morn.

"At the base of the knolls he encountered a tumbledown stake-and-rider fence. From the look of it he judged it must be forty years old at least—the work of some first pioneer who had taken up the land when the days of gold had ended. The woods were very thick here, yet fairly clear of underbrush, so that, while the blue sky was screened by the arched branches, he was able to ride beneath. He now found himself in a nook of several acres, where the oak and manzanita and madrono gave way to clusters of stately redwoods. Against the foot of a steep-sloped knoll he came upon a magnificent group of redwoods that seemed to have gathered about a tiny gurgling spring.

"He halted his horse, for beside the spring uprose a wild California lily.

It was a wonderful flower, growing there in the cathedral nave of lofty trees. At least eight feet in height, its stem rose straight and slender, green and bare, for two-thirds its length, and then burst into a shower of snow-white waxen bells. There were hundreds of these blossoms, all from the one stem, delicately poised and ethereally frail. Daylight had never seen anything like it. Slowly his gaze wandered from it to all that was about him. He took off his hat, with almost a vague religious feeling. This was different. No room for contempt and evil here. This was clean and fresh and beautiful—something he could respect. It was like a church. The atmosphere was one of holy calm. Here man felt the promptings of nobler things. Much of this and more was in Daylight's heart as he looked about him. But it was not a concept of his mind. He merely felt it without thinking about it at all.

"On the steep incline above the spring grew tiny maiden-hair ferns, while higher up were larger ferns and brakes. Great, moss-covered trunks of fallen trees lay here and there, slowly sinking back and merging into the level of the forest mould. Beyond, in a slightly clearer space, wild grape and honeysuckle swung in green riot from gnarled old oak trees. A gray Douglas squirrel crept out on a branch and watched him. From somewhere came the distant knocking of a woodpecker. This sound did not disturb the hush and awe of the place. Quiet woods' noises belonged there and made the solitude complete. The tiny bubbling ripple of the spring and the gray flash of tree-squirrel were as yardsticks with which to measure the silence and motionless repose.

" 'Might be a million miles from anywhere,' Daylight whispered to himself.

"But ever his gaze returned to the wonderful lily beside the bubbling spring.

"He tethered the horse and wandered on foot among the knolls. Their tops were crowned with century-old spruce trees, and their sides clothed with oaks and madronos and native holly. But to the perfect redwoods belonged the small but deep canyon that threaded its way among the knolls. Here he found no passage out for his horse, and he returned to the lily beside the spring. On foot, tripping, stumbling, leading the animal, he forced his way up the hillside. And ever the ferns carpeted the way of his feet, ever the forest climbed with him and arched overhead, and ever the clean joy and sweetness stole in upon his senses.

"On the crest he came through an amazing thicket of velvet-trunked

which his horse dropped slowly, with circumspect feet and reluctant gait."

I have quoted thus liberally from London's own descriptions that my readers might know something of the delight and charm of the place he has bought, and also of what my Boston friend was to enjoy.

Purposely I placed him next to London as we rode, and one can well understand what a delightful saddle companion he was. With that unusually keen power of observation of his, with an appreciation of beauty equal to his powers of observation; alive to the finger tips to every impression of

The sleeping mountain lake on the London Ranch, Valley of the Moon.

young madronos, and emerged on an open hillside that led down into a tiny valley. The sunshine was at first dazzling in its brightness, and he paused and rested, for he was panting from the exertion. Not of old had he known shortness of breath such as this and muscles that so easily tired at a stiff climb. A tiny stream ran down the tiny valley through a tiny meadow that was carpeted knee-high with grass and blue and white nemophila. The hillside was covered with Mariposa lilies and wild hyacinth, down through

joy or beauty; thoroughly informed on trees, plants, flowers, animals, birds, fishes and instincts, and gifted with unusual imagination, he fairly deluged my friend with his vivid and intense descriptions. It was needless for him to tell me how much he enjoyed it. I could tell by the rapid fire of question and answer, expression and reply, how eagerly he was taking it in. And it certainly was a morning ride fit for the gods, one of incomparable charm and exquisite delight.

Returned to the house, we had music from voice, piano and Victrola, and Jack related a number of interesting stories in connection with his trip on the "Snark." But more than all, I wanted my friend to see the intellectual workings of London's mind, so I started arguments with him on sociological questions. I aroused him enough by antagonism to stimulate his natural eloquence. Naturally, my friend prodded him also, for he prided himself upon his wide reading of all the schools of sociology. When I had got the two head over heels into red-hot debate, I let them "go it," hammer and tongs, for I knew what the result would be. London's memory seldom fails him, and his reading was as four to one compared with that of the Eastern scholar. The result was the latter found himself utterly unable to hold his own, and yet in his defeat felt that peculiar consciousness of pride that only a well educated man can feel, viz., that it has taken a man wonderfully well equipped with natural endowment and extraordinary reading to be able to cope with him.

The day was gone all too soon. After a tasty dinner the cart was brought and as we rode out to the train I turned and asked: "Well, how is it?" And then, for an hour, I listened to the Boston man's superlative expressions of the situation, the gist of which was as follows: "Why, sir, that man's life is the most ideal life of any literary man I know. His home is as near to perfection as I have ever seen a home and his companionship with his wife is something wonderful. It does not require any intelligence to discover the secret of his immense capacity for work. He is living in an artistic atmosphere, every element of which is perfectly congenial. And think of that ride! What a joy and privilege to have been able to take it with him! I never heard any one who so thoroughly entered into the spirit of Nature and the beauty of things as did this man who has always been described to me as so rude and primitive as to be absolutely brutal." And a great deal more along the same line.

And there, dear reader, you have it. Contact with London reveals him what my Boston friend discovered him to be. Whatever one's opinions of his sociological ideas, or of his literary work may be, his home life to-day is a very beautiful one, and his devotion to his wife, as also to his art, sincere and true.

Now let me attempt a description of the house that struck my Boston friend as so marvelously adapted to its requirements as a home and equally well fitted to its environment.

If in the building of a home the builders should express themselves, then Jack and Charmian London are building one of the most individualistic homes in the world. It is located on the London ranch in the Sonoma Valley—the valley of the moon, as the poetic Indian name suggests. Since his first land purchase he has bought two or three other adjoining ranches, until now the estate comprises about twelve hundred acres. Of this, nearly eight hundred acres are wild hillside and four hundred are under cultivation. With a glorious outlook on all four sides over fertile fields, with woods and mountain slopes, the house is being built on a knoll, with a most picturesque clump of redwoods at the back. Being out-of-door people, fond of water, the home is built around a patio, in the center of which is a water pool or tank of solid concrete forty by fifteen feet and six feet deep, fed by water from a cold mountain spring, and in which black bass will be kept, and where one may occasionally take a plunge—if he is brave and hardy enough.

Weeks have been spent upon the concrete bed which is practically the foundation of the house. Mr. London has here carried out an idea of his own, viz., that in an earthquake country as California, a house designed to be permanent should be especially guarded in its foundation. He reasons that a house built on a gigantic slab of concrete will move as a unit, and not one wall incline in one direction and another in the opposite direction when the quake occurs. Anyhow the architect has supervised the putting in of a bed of concrete sufficiently deep, thick and strong to sustain a forty-story skyscraper on a sandy foundation.

The architect is Mr. Albert Farr of San Francisco, a man of knowledge, experience and imagination, and as soon as Mr. and Mrs. London laid before him their ideas, he went to work to materialize them. The house is built chiefly of five materials, all of which are local products—redwood trees, a deep chocolate-maroon volcanic rock, blue slate, boulders and concrete. The London ranch furnishes the redwoods which are to be used with their jackets on, the rough deep-red colored bark harmonizing perfectly with the rough rock of the foundation. The rock is used exactly as blasted. It is not quarried in the sense of being worked regularly. It is simply blasted out and some chunks weigh several hundred pounds, some merely a few pounds and some as much as a ton or more. Just as they come they are hauled and placed in appropriate places. The result is immensely effective and attractive. The first floor is already built so that the effect is definitely known, and can be properly estimated. This house is ⌐—⌐ shaped, the main portion being eighty-six feet wide, with two eighty-two feet wings. The concrete water tank occupies the center of the patio, or open court. Around the tank will be a five-foot strip of garden, and this is the only piece of formal or conventional flower garden on the estate. Balconies built of redwood trunks are to surround the court.

The steps leading to the second story and the second story itself are to be built of the great boulders or cobble stones found on the estate, also the outside chimneys, and a builder has been found whose artistic work in the handling of these boulders is a joy and a delight.

The rough tree trunks will form the architectural lines of the porte-cochere, pergolas and porches, while the rafters are to be hewn out of rough redwood logs and kept in the natural finish. A charming effect is to be obtained by interlacing the tree trunks in the gables and balconies with fruit tree twigs. The roof will be of Spanish tile, colored to harmonize with the maroon of the rock and the redwood.

The interior is to be finished after the same rustic and individualistic fashion. It is to be essentially a home for the two people who are building it —a workshop for Mr. London, a home for Mrs. London, and a place where they can gather and entertain their friends. Hence these three ideas have been kept distinctly in the foreground. Mr. London's workroom is on the second floor, and is to be a magnificent room, nineteen by forty feet, with the library, exactly the same size, directly underneath, and the two connected with a spiral staircase. These two rooms are entirely apart from the rest of the house, thus affording perfect seclusion to the author while engaged at his work. His regular habit is to get to writing directly after breakfast, and he never writes less than one thousand words, his regular daily stunt. If this requires five hours, six, nine or merely two, it is always accomplished, and then the rest of the day is given over to hospitality, recreation or farming.

The chief feature of the house is the great living room, eighteen by fifty-eight feet, and extending over two stories high, with rough redwood balconies extending around the second floor. Open rafers for ceiling and gables, and an immense stone fireplace, which will be fed daily with gigantic logs from the woods on the estate, will give it a cheerful, homelike, though vast and medieval appearance.

The entrance way begins between two gigantic redwoods—and then leads to the porte-cochere, a roomy place big enough for the handling of the largest touring cars.

Immediately from the porte-cochere one enters the large hall, which, except for massive, handsomely wrought iron gates, will be perpetually open, reaching completely from the front to the rear of the building. From this hall three large guest rooms, the patio and the author's workshop are reached on the left hand side, and on the right a reception room, with coat rooms, toilets and all conveniences, a gun-room, the stairs and the large living room. One of the two large alcoves of the living room is to be especially arranged for Mrs. London's Steinway grand piano, a kingly instrument, which gives her intense pleasure, and which will assuredly afford great joy and entertainment to her guests.

Long ago Mr. and Mrs. London fully decided the question that city life had not enough compensations to offer for home life. So they are building with this thought in view—to make a home for themselves where they can welcome and entertain all the friends they desire. They both laugh heartily at the comment of a city lady who, visiting the growing house and not knowing that any one could hear her, exclaimed: "What fools they are! building such a glorious house where none can see it!" as if the chief end of building a home was for "some one to see it." The Londons have a right appreciation of values, and they know how to place things. The first requirement of a house is that it shall be a home for those who are to live in it—the appreciation of others is a secondary consideration. From this viewpoint the London house will be ideal.

It is to contain its own hot water, heating, electric lighting, refrigerating, vacuum cleaning and laundry plants—the latter with steam dryer rotary wringer—a milk and store room, root and wine cellar.

Its name is "Wolf House," a reminder of London's book plate which is the big face of a wolf dog, and of his first great literary success, "The Call of the Wild."

At present the Londons are living in a group of the old houses they found on the estate. It has been renovated, fixed over, added to, repainted and refurnished, and it makes a most comfortable home until the new one is completed. How long that will be Jack laughingly declares no one knows —as he stops building as soon as his money gives out. So he and his mate are enjoying the building more than most people enjoy such work, one reason, doubtless, being because of this element of uncertainty.

In my personal touches with London he reveals more and more of the philosophy that controls him. One day we were talking about what life is, and what its conflicts mean, and he said in effect:

"I judge my life largely by the victories I have been able to gain! The things I remember best are my great victories. Two of these were won when I was a very small child, and one was won in a dream. When I was about three years old we were moving from one part of Oakland to another. Up to that time I had not known fear, but this particular afternoon when I went into the house and saw the vacant rooms, the boxes and furniture moved here and there, and everything different, and suddenly realized that I was alone in the house, a deadly fear came upon me. I was in a room one window of which looked out into a yard where some of the folks were beating carpets, and with this horrible dread upon me, unable to call out, afraid, I suppose, to do so, I could only find relief in going to the window and looking out. I thought of running to those outside, but one look into the room, and realizing that I had to go through two rooms before I reached the outside door, effectually deterred me. For awhile I succeeded in beating down the fear. Then, suddenly, I realized that the carpet beating was stopped and the folks had gone somewhere, that I was entirely alone, and that it was twilight and night was speedily coming down with its dark pall. For awhile I was terror-stricken and I suffered more torture than even now I care to recall. But by and by I braced up and resolutely I determined to face the terror. Gathering myself together, bracing up my will, I sturdily walked through the rooms to the outside, feeling the thrill of victory as I did so.

"My other childish victory was over a peculiar nightmare. I had lived in the country and was one day brought to town and stood on a railway platform as a railway engine came in. Its ponderous size, its easy and resistless onward movement, its panting, its fire and smoke, its great noises, all impressed me so powerfully that that night I dreamed of it, and when the dream turned to a nightmare was filled with dread and horror at what seemed to be the fact that this locomotive was pursuing me and that I could not get out of its way. For weeks thereafter I was haunted by this dreadful fear, and night after night I was run down. But, strange to say, I always rose up again after suffering the pangs of a horrible death, to go over it all again. The torture those nightmares gave me none can understand except those who have gone through a similar experience. Then one night came release. In the distance, as the mighty modern Juggernaut came towards me, I saw a man with a stepladder. I was unable to cry out, but I waved my hand to him. He hailed me and bade me come. That broke the spell. I ran to him, climbed to the top of the stepladder, and thereafter lost all terror at the sight of a locomotive. But the victory gained in climbing the ladder was as real as any I ever had in my waking life.

"Another victory was gained when I learned that fame didn't count, and another when I learned that I could do without money. To-day I could look upon the loss of all my income with equanimity, for I know I have strength enough to go out and earn enough for Charmian and me to live on healthfully and simply. Another was when I ceased to fear death, and one of my latest triumphs was the victory gained over my dread of death by a knife. I have always had a terror of being killed by cutting with a knife. Often have I faced death, in a variety of ways, but an open knife always gave me the horrors. After I got up

from the hospital in Australia, when we decided to give up the Snark trip, I had a five weeks' growth of heavy moustache and beard. I went to a barber's, where there were eight chairs, took my seat and the barber began. After he had lathered me and taken off a part of my beard, I suddenly noticed that the hand that rested on me was shaking frightfully. I looked and saw the razor hand approaching me, but jerking, as if the man was in a fit. It barely touched my skin when he drew it back. At first I was speechless with fright. A panic seized me, and I wanted to jump up and rush out. Then I pulled myself together and asked what it all meant. I recalled to my mind the mental conflicts I had recently had while face to face with myself on the hospital cot. What did all my arguments and assertions as to the supremacy of mind over body really mean. Here was an opportunity to test them. I could dodge the issue by slipping into another seat. But I determined to test myself. Quietly looking up, I asked the barber: 'What's up?' He answered in effect that he had been out with the boys on Saturday night—this was Monday—and for the first time in his life his dissipation had produced the 'shakes.' In a hoarse whisper he begged me not to give him away, as that would mean losing his job, and places were scarce just then.

"'Take your time,' I said; 'I'll give you a chance, but be careful.'

"Then for fully three-quarters of an hour I waited and watched that fellow —his hand shaking uncontrollably— bring that razor to my cheek, lip or chin, knowing that a moment's shake at the wrong time might mean the taking off of a piece of me.

"That I call a great victory."

As throwing small sidelights upon London's inner thoughts, the following may assist. They are the inscriptions written by his own hand in the various books he has sent me:

In the "People of the Abyss"; "Walk with me here, among the creatures damned by man, and then wonder not that I sign myself, Yours for the Revolution."

In "Children of the Frost": "Find herein *my* Indians; I imagine they do not differ very much from *yours*."

In his "War of the Classes" he wrote: "Read here some of the reasons of my socialism, and some of my socialism."

In another copy of "The War of the Classes," knowing that I was a continuous student of Browning, he wrote: "God's still in his heaven, but all's not well with the world."

How suggestive this from "The Kempton-Wace Letters": "I'd rather be ashes than dust."

In "Tales of the Fish Patrol": "Find within these pages my youthful stamping ground, when I first went 'on my own' into the world."

In "The Sea Wolf": "Find here, in the mouth of the Sea Wolf, much of the philosophy that was mine in my 'long sickness.' It is still mine, though now that I am happy, I keep it covered over with veils of illusion."

The chief character in this book is Wolf Larsen. He is a wonderful conception, wonderfully drawn, a strong and impelling character, a human being devoid of all morality, all sentiment, save that of living solely for his own pleasure and interest. He is pictured as being neither moral nor immoral, simply unmoral, knowing no standard of right and wrong, recognizing no impelling duty save that of personal interest. He is the incarnation of materialism and selfish individualism, which, as London says above, was for a time his "great sickness."

Yet he is made the instrument for good. It would be immeasurably better for the individual, and therefore for the race, if all the "Sissies" and "Miss Nancys," the bloodless, super-refined, super-sensitive, super-civilized creatures of the Van Weyden type were compelled to undergo some such treatment as Wolf Larsen gave to him. In the Wolf's words they would learn to "stand upon their own legs" instead of walking upon those of

their fathers. "The Sea Wolf" clearly teaches Jack London's philosophies upon this subject. Van Weyden, the scholar and dilettante, says of himself: "I had never done any hard manual labor or scullion labor in my life. I had lived a placid, uneventful, sedentary existence all my days—the life of a scholar and a recluse on an assured and comfortable income. Violent life and athletic sports had never appealed to me. I had always been a bookworm; so my sisters and my father had called me during my childhood. I had gone camping but once in my life, and then I left the party almost at the start and returned to the comforts and conveniences of a roof. And here I was, with dreary and endless vistas before me of table setting, potato peeling and dish washing, and I was not strong. The doctors had always said that I had a remarkable constitution, but I had never developed it or my body through exercise. My muscles were small and soft like a woman's, or so the doctors had said time and again in the course of their attempts to persuade me to go in for physical culture fads. But I had preferred to use my head rather than my body; and here I was, in no fit condition for the rough life in prospect."

There you have it: a dreamy, sensuous, half life he had lived, his body rusting and rotting for want of use. How could health of thought come from such a body? Half the thought that controls the world is diseased thought, rotten thought, born of diseased and rotten bodies. For thought to be strong and virile and pure it must come through strong, virile and pure bodies. The man who lives a lazy, selfish, self-indulgent life cannot think other than lazy, selfish, self-indulgent thoughts. And it was the mission of Wolf Larsen, cruel, horrible, terrible though it seemed at first to Humphrey Van Weyden, to show him the uselessness and inutility of his own life, the helplessness of it and to develop within him powers of usefulness, or self-reliance, of mental grasp. As you read of Van Weyden's treatment your blood boils at times with anger and indignation, yet the ultimate outcome was good, in the highest degree good. It taught the hitherto useless and selfish man a sympathy with the hard and cruel work of others; it developed his body, his mind, his invention, his soul. See him there, as London pictures him, when cast ashore on Endeavor Island, with the woman he loved, struggling with the masts of the dismasted "Ghost" in order that he may get back to civilization. Day after day he grapples with problems of weight, levers, fulcrums, blocks and tackles, and little by little knows the joy of overcoming them. He learns what it is to really live—to live in active battling with the real problems that meet men and women in real life. So, in the end, one is forced to the conclusion that his experiences were good for him in every way. They had made a man of him—a real man, not a semblance of a man. A self-reliant, self-competent, self-dependent man, full of sympathy for his fellows, knowing the hardships and difficulties of their lives and realizing the joys of their triumphs. And to be a man is much. Welcome the teacher, hard though he be, that teaches us manhood.

So Jack London's book comes to me with the highest sanction. It teaches human puppets to be men through the strenuous endeavor of compelling life.

In his later books his humor asserts itself more than formerly. He is far more jolly, human and humorous than most of his readers conceive. For instance, when he was living at Wake Robin Lodge, where I first met him, he had a notice on the front door of his library or studio: "No Admittance Except on Business!" Then underneath, "Positively no Business Transacted Here." On the back door were these legends: "No one admitted without knocking." "Please do not knock."

Yet it cannot be denied that humor is a secondary or tertiary thing to him. He has been compelled by the hard knocks of life to be so deadly in earnest, and he has so thoroughly taken upon himself the burden of the downtrodden classes that, while he fully appreciates humor, can tell a good story and laughs as heartily as any man, the serious side of life is ever uppermost to him.

This is clearly seen in the concluding words of his compelling paper, "What Life Means to Me." He there says:

"I discovered that I did not like to live on the parlor floor of society. Intellectually I was bored. Morally and spiritually I was sickened. I remembered my intellectuals and idealists, my unfrocked preachers, broken professors, and clean-minded, class conscious workingmen. I remembered my days and nights of sunshine and starshine, where life was all a wild, sweet wonder, a spiritual paradise of unselfish adventure and ethical romance. And I saw before me, ever blazing and burning, the Holy Grail.

"So I went back to the working class in which I had been born and where I belonged. I care no longer to climb. The imposing edifice of society above my head holds no delights for me. It is the foundation of the edifice that interests me. There I am content to labor, crowbar in hand, shoulder to shoulder with intellectuals, idealists and class-conscious workingmen, getting a solid pry now and again and setting the whole edifice rocking. Some day, when we get a few more hands and crowbars to work, we'll topple it over, along with all its rotten life and unburied dead, its monstrous selfishness and sodden materialism. Then we'll cleanse the cellar and build a new habitation for mankind, in which there will be no parlor floor, in which all the rooms will be bright and airy, and where the air that is breathed will be clean, noble and alive.

"Such is my outlook. I look forward to a time when man shall progress upon something worthier and higher than his stomach, when there will be a finer incentive to impel men to action than the incentive of to-day, which is the incentive of the stomach. I retain my belief in the nobility and excellence of the human. I believe that spiritual sweetness and unselfishness will conquer the gross gluttony of to-day. And, last of all, my faith is in the working class. As some Frenchman has said: 'The stairway of time is ever echoing with the wooden shoe going up, the polished boot descending.' "

Let me here say a few words as to London's socialism.

It is useless to say that his theories and ideas are impracticable. It is impossible to ignore them. He and his compeers argue with relentless logic that will not be gainsaid. The capitalistic class, they say, has had up to now the management of the affairs of the world. The laboring class, perforce, has had to accept this management, live by the laws the capitalists have formulated, accept the wages paid, pay the prices demanded for rents, commodities, clothing and food, and live in rigid conformity to the will of the capitalists—as expressed in the laws and in social requirements—with little more than a pretended voice of suggestion in the making of these laws. They openly claim that this management has been a failure as far as the higher development of mankind is concerned. They point with bitterness to the evidences of material and financial prosperity side by side with increasing misery and wretchedness and the growing fierceness of the struggle for existence. In his essay entitled "Revolution," London compares the existence of the cave-man with the conditions of life among the poor to-day, and calls upon the poor to assert their rights, show their power at the ballot-box and claim their own. The red banner, by the way, symbolizes the brotherhood of man and does not symbolize the incendiarism that instantly connects itself with the red banner in the affrighted bourgeois mind. The comradeship of the revolutionists is alive and warm. It passes over geographical lines, transcends race prejudice, and has even proven itself mightier than the Fourth of July, spread-eagle Americanism of our forefathers. The French socialist working-men and the German socialist workingmen forget Alsace and Lorraine, and, when war threatens, pass resolutions declaring that as workingmen and comrades, they have no quarrel with each other. When Japan and Russia sprang at each other's throats, the revolutionists of Japan addressed the following message to the revolutionists of Russia:

"Dear Comrades: Your government and ours have recently plunged into war to carry out their imperialistic tendencies, but for us socialists there are no boundaries, race, country, nationality. We are comrades, brothers and sisters, and have no reason to fight. Your enemies are not the Japanese people, but our militarism and socalled patriotism. Patriotism and militarism are our mutual enemies."

Here is another utterance that should be calmly weighed and duly considered:

"One thing must be clearly understood. This is no spontaneous and vague uprising of a large mass of discontented and miserable people—a blind and instinctive recoil from trust. On the contrary, the propaganda is intellectual; the movement is based upon economic necessity and is in line with social evolution; while the miserable people have not yet revolted. The revolutionist is no starved and diseased slave in the shambles at the bottom of the social pit, but is, in the main, a hearty, well fed workingman who sees the shambles waiting for him and his children and declines to descend. The very miserable people are too helpless to help themselves. But they are being helped, and the day is not far distant when their numbers will go to swell the ranks of the revolutionists."

There are those who ask, Why exploit the socialistic ideas of London? Is there not something of the ostrich hiding its head in the sand in this mental attitude? If socialism is dangerous, the sooner we who profess to be less radical know it the better. Let us fully understand the ideas, the propaganda, the methods these men and women have in their minds; then, if they are to be combatted, we can the more intelligently go to work to combat them. But to shut our eyes and ears, to remain wilfully blind and deaf until the storm is upon us is both foolish, absurd and suicidal.

About five years ago on one of my visits to Glen Ellen, Jack and his wife were full of their contemplated trip on "The Snark." They had decided to make it, and Jack and "Roscoe" spent hours going over their plans. I used to watch and listen and enjoy it all in anticipation with them. They planned to be gone for seven years, to circumnavigate the globe and visit every place that appealed to them.

A few days after I left them I wrote the following, gendered by the unfolding of London's philosophy as it appeared to me at the time:

"Seven years on a small vessel, journeying through storms and calms, in all kinds of seas in all kinds of weathers. Seven years of risk, of uncertainty, of danger—so it appears to a landsman. But how does it seem to him? Read his stories of the Fish Patrol in San Francisco harbor; get it well into your understanding that as a lad of sixteen he was the hero of adventure, of daring and bravery that were taken as the everyday work of capturing desperate and armed men who violated the laws of the Fish Commissioners; men who defiantly pirated the oyster beds; men to whom the sailing of their vessels in all weathers and in the fogs and darkness of night was part of their everyday life; men whose whole lives had been spent on the sea—I say he entered into the task of foiling these men in their illegal work when but a mere lad of sixteen. With his superior, or alone, he sailed the vessel of the fish patrol and sought to outsail and outwit defiant and mocking men. Here, then, was his school. Here was his training ground. As you read his fish and sea stories you see that the uncertain deck of the tossing vessel, the uprearing and downfalling of the ship as it is lifted by the wild and boisterous waves is a place of sure footing to him. Masts

and sails and oars and tackles and keels and center-boards and the like are all as familiar to him as fashions are to the dude, and not in a dilettante way, but in the stern, real, positive way that comes in the discharge of arduous, wearisome, dangerous and exciting daily labor.

"His, therefore, will be no amateur trip. He knows what he is about. He is an expert sailor. He as thoroughly understands the handling and working of a vessel as an expert mechanic trained as a chauffeur understands the manipulation of an automobile.

"And yet more than this is necessary for the *master* of a vessel. He must understand the art of navigation. That is, he must understand not only all about the actual working of the vessel, but how to determine his course in the night, in a fog, how to find his location when wind, adverse current and storm have forced him out of his expected path. This knowledge he does not possess. But this is no real obstacle. Here is where his superb mental training and self-discipline come in. He knows that a few days' reading up will give him the scientific knowledge necessary to learn these things. What a school man must spend months to learn, he knows that his well-disciplined intellect, with its powers of concentration, absorption and retention can master in a few weeks. So with supreme self-reliance he looks upon the necessary knowledge as almost attained, and goes on with his preparation without a flutter of fear at his heart."

London himself, in his book, "The Cruise of the Snark," enlarges upon this crude presentation of his ideas in the following vigorous fashion:

"The thing I like most of all is personal achievement—not achievement for the world's applause, but achievement for my own delight. It is the old 'I did it! I did it! With my own hands I did it!' But personal achievement, with me, must be concrete. I'd rather win a water-fight in the swimming pool, or remain astride a horse that is trying to get out from under me, than write the great American novel. Each man to his liking. Some other fellow would prefer writing the great Ameircan novel to winning the water-fight or mastering the horse.

"Possibly the proudest achievement of my life, my moment of highest living, occurred when I was seventeen. I was in a three-masted schooner off the coast of Japan. We were in a typhoon. All hands had been on deck most of the night. I was called from my bunk at seven in the morning to take the wheel. Not a stitch of canvas was set. We were running before it with bare poles, yet the schooner fairly tore along. The seas were all of an eighth of a mile apart, and the wind snatched the whitecaps from their summits, filling the air so thick with driving spray that it was impossible to see more than two waves at a time. The schooner was almost unmanageable, rolling her rail under to starboard and to port, veering and yawing anywhere between southeast and southwest, and threatening when the huge seas lifted under her quarter, to broach to. Had she broached to, she would ultimately have been reported with all hands and no tidings.

"I took the wheel. The sailing master watched me for a space. He was afraid of my youth, feared that I lacked the strength and the nerve. But when he saw me successfully wrestle the schooner through several bouts, he went below to breakfast. Fore and aft all hands were below at breakfast. Had she broached to, not one of them would ever have reached the deck. For forty minutes I stood there alone at the wheel, in my grasp the wildly careering schooner and the lives of twenty-two men. Once we were pooped. I saw it coming, and, half-drowned, with tons of water crushing me, I checked the schooner's rush to broach to. At the end of the hour, sweating and played out, I was relieved. But I had done it! With my own hands I had done the trick at the wheel and guided a hundred tons of wood and iron through a few million tons of wind and waves.

"My delight was in that I had done it—not in the fact that twenty-two men knew I had done it. Within the year over half of them were dead and gone, yet my pride in the thing performed was not diminished by half.

"Life that lives is life successful, and success is the breath of its nostrils. The achievement of a difficult feat is successful adjustment to a sternly exacting environment. The more difficult the feat, the greater the satisfaction at its accomplishment. Thus it is with the man who leaps forward from the springboard, out over the swimming pool, and with a backward half-revolution of the body, enters the water head first. Once he left the springboard his environment was immediately savage, and savage the penalty it would have exacted had he failed and struck the water flat. Of course, the man did not have to run the risk of the penalty. He could have remained on the bank in a sweet and placid environment of summer air, sunshine and stability. Only he was not made that way. In the swift mid-air moment he lived as he could never have lived on the bank.

"The trip around the world means big moments of living. Bear with me a moment, and look at it. Here am I, a little animal called a man—a bit of vitalized matter, one hundred and sixty-five pounds of meat and blood, nerve, sinew, bones and brain—all of it soft and tender, susceptible to hurt, fallible and frail. I strike a light back-handed blow on the nose of an obstreperous horse, and a bone in my hand is broken. I put my head under the water for five minutes and I am drowned. I fall twenty feet through the air and I am smashed. I am a creature of temperature. A few degrees one way and my fingers and toes blacken and drop off. A few degrees the other way, and my skin blisters and shrivels away from the raw, quivering flesh. A few additional degrees either way, and the life and the light in me go out. A drop of poison injected into my body from a snake, and I cease to move—forever I cease to move. A splinter of lead from a rifle enters my head, and I am wrapped around in the eternal blackness.

"Fallible and frail, a bit of pulsating, jelly-like life—it is all I am. About me are the great natural forces—colossal menaces, Titans of destruction, unsentimental monsters that have less concern for me than I have for the grain of sand I crush under my foot. They have no concern at all for me. They do not know me. They are unconscious, unmerciful and unmoral. They are the cyclones and tornadoes, lightning flashes and cloud-bursts, tide-rips and tidal waves, under-tows and waterspouts, great whirls and sucks and eddies, earthquakes and volcanoes, surfs that thunder on rock-ribbed coasts and seas that leap aboard the largest crafts that float, crushing humans to pulp or licking them off into the sea and to death—and these insensate monsters do not know that tiny sensitive creature, all nerves and weaknesses, whom men call Jack London, and who himself thinks he is all right and quite a superior being.

"In the maze and chaos of the conflict of these vast and draughty Titans, it is for me to thread my precarious way. The bit of life that is I will exult over them. The bit of life that is I, in so far as it succeeds in baffling them or in bidding to its service, will imagine that it is godlike. It is good to ride the tempest and feel godlike. I dare to assert that for a finite speck of pulsating jelly to feel godlike is a far more glorious feeling than for a god to feel godlike.

"Here is the sea, the wind and the wave. Here are the seas, the winds and the waves of all the world. Here is ferocious environment. And here is difficult adjustment, the achievement of which is delight to the small quivering vanity that is I. I like. I am so made. It is my own particular form of vanity, that is all."

They made a wonderful start and did some remarkable voyaging, all of which is told in graphic fashion in London's "Cruise of the Snark." But circumstances over which they had no control compelled the giving up of the trip when they reached Australia, and they returned to their home in Glen Ellen, there to furbish up the old ranch house, begin the building of the new and wonderful home, construct the trails and be happy, as I have described in the earlier pages of this already prolonged sketch. That they are not compulsorily anchored is evidenced by the fact that a few months ago they decided to take a trip to New York. While there, one or the other or both decided that a sailing vessel trip to California around Cape Horn would suit them, and in twenty-four hours arrangements were made and they were off.

Whatever else may be said of London, no one can truthfully say of him that he has not lived. In his less than forty years of life he has played on a gamut of several octaves, and from present indication life is just as intense, as vivid, and as full with him as when he fought his battle with the bully newsboy on the streets of Oakland, or the bully sailor on the deck of the Behring Sea whaler.

He is very much alive.

Jack London

An Appreciation

Here' to you, Jack, whose virile pen
Concerns itself with Man's Size Men;
Here's to you, Jack, whose stories thrill
    With savor of the Western breeze,
With magic of the south—and chill,
    Shrill winds from icy floes and seas,
YOU have not wallowed in the mire
And muck of tales of foul desire,
For, though you've sung of fight and fraud,
    Of love and hate—ashore, afloat—
    You have not struck a ribald note,
Nor made your Art a common bawd.

Here's to you, Jack, I've loved your best,
    Your finest stories from the first,
Your sagas of the North and West—
    But what is more—I've loved your Worst!
For, in the poorest work you do,
There's something clean and strong and true,
A tang of big and primal things,
    A sweep of forces vast and free,
A touch of wizardry which brings
    The glamour of the Wild to me.

So when I read a London tale,
    Forthwith I'm set upon a trail
Of great enchantment, and track
Adventure round the world and back,
With you for guide—here's to you, Jack.
BERTON BRALEY.

Mrs. Jack London's New Viewpoint

By L. Rudio Marshall

AS I STEPPED from the carriage that brought me from Glen Ellen to the vine-covered home on the London ranch in the Valley of the Moon, a bright sunbeam seemed to slip out of the door and greet me with the informal kindliness of a young girl. In the delightful feeling of this cordial spirit of pure friendliness I realized the full meaning of the old-time saying of Jack's friends: "Jack's home is the real home." The trail to that home is well worn with footprints, and is an ever-ready remembrance to his hosts of staunch friends in all quarters of the globe. Perhaps there is no place of its kind in the West that has attracted so many and such a variety of visitors as the Home That Jack Built with the latch string always hanging out—and beckoning.

"It is so good of you to come," Mrs. London exclaimed warmly, making me completely at home with her radiant kindliness. "There is so much to tell and I know that you will enjoy yourself. Come in and let me make you comfortable."

After we had chatted awhile in a lovely arcade overlooking a glorious panoramic view of the valley, backed by the rising hills, she began in low tones: "I will carry out Jack's work as he planned it. He left behind enough material to write books for at least one hundred years."

She reached to a shelf nearby, which was covered with scattered photographs. "Here are Jack and I at Honolulu. Here we are in the Sierras." She shuffled many photographs, all depicting Jack and herself in many places in the Western world. Occasionally she paused meditatively over a picture that recalled some striking incident in their far-ranging journeys into happiness. She held a bunch of photographs close to her and said, brightly: "I believe that Jack is always with me. I live and hope under that impression. He would wish it, I know, and I love the idea."

We talked of his early work and how, after persistent and desperate endeavors, he at last "found himself" and attained the first recognition through publication in Overland Monthly, oddly enough the magazine founded by Bret Harte, in 1868, to furnish a vehicle whereby California writers might be developed.

London's first contribution to Overland was the five "Malemute Kid" series, "The Son of the Wolf," etc., beginning January, 1899, all dealing with his then recent Alaskan experiences.

Mrs. London selected several photographs and handed them to me. "Take them to Overland Monthly," she said, "as a compliment to the management for what it did to start Jack on his literary career."

After the publication of these Alaskan stories, London's further contributions were readily accepted by Eastern publishers, and his success widened with each story printed.

Later I was invited by Mrs. Shepard —Jack London's sister and manager of the ranch—to take a stroll and become better acquainted with the sequestered trails and the roads threading the woodland slopes and the glorious prospect they offered. Mrs. Shepard showed all the supple and exhilarating signs of outdoor life. Being in ideal physical condition, she promptly developed into one of the most enthusiastic and persistent walkers I ever hope to keep pace with. An invitation to join her for a little ramble, "just to view some of the more captivating prospects," is doing a marathon for which one should be crowned as in the Olympian games.

It was Jack London's spurring ambition to make his extensive land-holding of hill and dale provide everything needful for its consumption and use. Independence was his motto. Along this line he had developed his plans to a point where he was preparing to inaugurate his own school house for the benefit of the many children on the ranch, as well as his own store, furnished with all kinds of merchandise for the numerous families employed, and a post-office. With his ardent enthusiasm he was always planning new benefits for the workers around him, heartfelt endeavors to ameliorate their condition and educate them to advantages superior to any they might attain under their own initiative.

Jack never skimped on any cost that might make his holding more attractive. So when he decided to have a colorful background of Western bronco busters on his range, he brought out a number of real thoroughbred cowboys from Cheyenne, headed by a genius in that line, named Hayes. London loved horses, and the pride and gem of the display on his ranch was the prize stallion, Neuadd Hillside. Singularly enough Jack died on the 22d of the month; so did the stallion on the same date of the preceding mouth, and the ambitious House That Jack Built, his famous castle, burned down on the 22d, some three years prior.

On my hike with Mrs. Shepard, we gradually threaded the main departments of the ranch, the storehouse, blacksmith shop, the cool rooms of the dairy and the specklessly clean slaughter house, where the animals are killed and dressed to supply the families working on the place. Then by easy ascent we climbed the wooded trails, and as we turned a corner of trees, a gem-like lake, an exquisite

mirror reflecting the heavens and the serenity of the picturesque scene, came suddenly into view. Later, Mrs. London told me of the profound affection she and Jack entertained for that sacred little spot, the site where they and their most intimate friends spent many happy evening hours with the canopy of stars overhead and the gently nodding sentinel trees looking approval.

There is where Jack took his cronies when they came up from San Francisco, Oakland and other places for a "time." Hampers of food were carried along, and drinkables. Fish were caught from the lake and popped into a hot pan and crackling potatoes seared with the coals were raked out as they reached the point of bursting like a boll of cotton. And as the good fellows and their mates stretched out before the glowing embers of the big log fire, the stars gradually faded while the talk ranged its devious way round the circle, weird experiences, wonderful adventures, the pet theories of philosophers, prophets and radicals, the uncanny rim of life, freedom of the will, revelations of their wildest and most fantastic dreams—a mental giant swing to loop the loop between a Walpurgis night and the Miltonian heavens. Jack's wolves and elemental humans, the while fantastically threading the themes of discussion.

From an eminence near the lake, Mrs. Shepard pointed out a hillside with terrace after terrace dropping stairwise down the slope.

"There you see one of Jack's many striking hobbies," she explained— "terrace farming. When Jack bought these 1,500 acres they had been abandoned by six different ranchers, and each had done his level best to exhaust the soil and squeeze it of the last profit possible, till the ground was as sterile as a piece of cement. Jack attacked the problem with his usual zeal, and by degrees stimulated the impoverished soil with proper nutritives. There you see the result of his efforts, an abundant profitable crop. Along this line, Jack's ambition was to develop a model farm; one of the best all-round ranches in the State, combining a stock ranch, fruit, grain, vegetables, vineyard and the like. He would have accomplished his plan had he lived, for his enthusiasm was unquenchable. His intense energy simply rioted in work. Success seemed only to stimulate him to greater and wider efforts."

By this time, being somewhat plump, I was becoming a bit nervous regarding the many surrounding hills about me which Mrs. Shepard seemed determined to climb in order to show me the many other interesting points. I suggested that for a change it might prove a relief to go down the hills instead of everlastingly climbing them. Apparently she did not catch my gasping hope, for suddenly she shot a sharp glance at me.

"You're a tenderfoot," she said. There was a twinkle in her eye and about the corners of her mouth a lurking expression of teasing.

"Yes," I replied, frankly. "My feet are tender, more tender than I ever suspected on such high hills."

She laughed. And later, when we reached the house, Mrs. London laughed too, when I caricatured my experiences in hillside climbing. She explained to me the extraordinary self service Jack's sister was doing for the ranch. Mrs. Shepard alone handles all the important business, crop problems and other responsibilities. The bungalow in which she lives is the business headquarters of the ranch. Mrs. Shepard is out and over the hills and the valley at all hours, looking sharply after the manifold details in the proper development of the ranch. She thinks nothing of a day's hike up hill and down dale, checking up the hands and the various special jobs scattered over the broad acreage. Aside from this she has the responsibility of watching market prices in order to dispose the crops at advantageous figures, the purchase of new machinery, agricultural implements, and the thousand and one things required on a ranch of such extent and possi-

bilities. By dealers she is accounted as a keenly competent woman. Mrs. Shepard was evidently born for the position, as she took to it like a duck to water. Five years ago she visited her brother's ranch for a month's vacation to recuperate her health. She has remained there ever since, an ideal overseer, enjoying to the full her healthy and happy capacity of "doing things well worth while."

We walked back to the London house, and there in a room I found Mrs. London combing over numberless relics which she and Jack had collected on the thousand and one journeys taken to divers places scattered about the world. Hundreds of pictures of Jack, it seemed to me, taken in various foreign garbs. Many of them were entitled "The Wolf," as Jack was familiarly called by those who knew him best. His laughing eyes peeped from all quarters of the room. Every glance by Mrs. London at "The Wolf" was an adoration.

Mrs. London picked up one of the photographs, kissed it fondly, and exclaimed: "Dear old Jack; no one knows how I miss him. What is the use of weeping and moping? He wouldn't want it. I shall always live in the way he would want me to."

And so she fills out her life in sincere effort to carry out the work left by him according to his ideas.

Presently she brought out one of her special treasures; her private copy of the "Log of the Snark," which she wrote on the notable voyage of that vessel to describe the happy trip she and her husband made in the South Seas; a book that throws more intimate light on their happy, buoyant life of camaraderie than can be found in all the other "London" books published. The volume is dedicated to Jack London, and was recently issued by the Macmillan Publishing Company, New York. It is Mrs. London's first attempt at authorship, and has proved a wonderful success because of its sincere naturalness and the delightful spirit which pervades it. In that book the reader sees and realizes the true

Jack London; his daily life is pictured familiarly, his writing hours, his day dreaming, his exuberant spirits and cosmic plans, his sincere thoughtfulness of his host of friends, his canny hunches, his aspirations, his plans for a tangible eternity, and the deep devotion between man and wife. He had a score of pet names for her, love names that he had selected: "Mate," "Mate Woman," "Crackerjack."

Every mail to Glen Ellen these days brings bundles of letters to Mrs. London congratulating her upon the immediate success of the "Log of the Snark." With beaming pride she read to me a letter written by a prominent publisher in Paris thanking her for an article she had recently written for him, and enclosing a check of cheerful figures, the first she had ever received. Laying down the letter she exclaimed radiantly: "My! Wouldn't Jack be proud of me?"

The remarkable success of Mrs. London's first book is an augury that many popular books from her pen will follow.

Jack died on a couch screened in on a wide porch overlooking a beautiful panoramic view of the Valley of the Moon, so appropriately named by him. All over his couch and about him were coverings of the wonderful collection of furs of wild animals he had gathered from the Western world.

Mrs. London walked over to a couch and pointed to a dial on the wooden frame above. "Dear Jack," she said; "for years he had set this alarm clock to strike at 6 a. m. See, the hour hand is now pointing at 8 o'clock. On the last night his strength failed, and for the first time in many years of his writing the dial was not set at 6 o'clock, his regular hour of rising.

"In one of the very last talks we had he expressed his deep sympathy for those in low circumstances who were striving with all kinds of shifts and economies to acquire a home. He had been considering plans to locate them on country land tracts. The problem had not been worked out in detail, but his persistent enthusiasm regarding it, during even his sickness, indicated how determined he was in efforts to materialize it. Jack was the incarnation of loyalty to a friend, and no matter what the friend's position was in the world, whether he lacked money, influence or position, or was a radical driven at bay, Jack had ever a ready hand to help him."

During the ebb and flow of his sinking spells, Jack became impressed with the idea that perhaps after all his rugged and robust constitution might not pull him through. At once he rigidly insisted that nobody should attend his funeral except his wife, his sister, Mrs. Shepard, and George Sterling, his fidue Achates, through years of hardship, toil and success, each recognizing the stable qualities of the other, and the genius.

Jack was buried on the spot which he had carefully selected a long time before; a spot commanding a sweeping view of the Valley of the Moon, and embracing the ruins of his beloved former home, so endearingly planned by his wife and himself, the House That Jack Built. A huge red stone boulder marks his resting place.

Later Mrs. London and I rambled along a smooth road with stately trees lining each side, and on a bend of the hillside we came out on a point overlooking the beautiful sweep of the ranch. In the middle distance were the ruins of the House That Jack Built, resembling the remains of an old castle that had already accumulated its legends. Mrs. London steadfastly regarded the beloved spot, lost in silence. Suddenly she shook her head: "I never would care to rebuild it," she said.

The site is on a noble eminence. I suggested that she should donate the place for a prominent State building as a memorial to Jack London. She had never thought of such a solution.

In considering the matter, I told her of a number of precedents where land had been donated by private parties to State institutions, notably to the University of California, where Jack London had been a student, and I recounted to her the great success the University was making on its farm at Davis, where students were trained in the practical details of various agricultural pursuits. And as I looked over the beautiful prospect, I felt that Jack London, with all his generosity and humanity, his deep concern to benefit his fellow men, would heartily approve the idea.

All Mrs. London's ideas are cradled in the thought of what Jack would want her to do. Jack keenly and appreciatively sensed how implicitly she would follow his pet views, and it followed naturally that practically the whole estate was bequeathed to his wife. Surely Jack London had every reason to call her his "Mate."

Aside from such plans, Mrs. Jack London is now bent on assisting as best she can in the education of her two step-daughters. It is known only to a very few of the most intimate friends that the Londons had a little baby girl, born in 1910. She lived only a few days. That was the only real sorrow that came into their lives.

JACK LONDON'S PLEA FOR THE SQUARE DEAL

Editor "The Overland Monthly."

Dear Sir:

At the present time I am undergoing a pirate raid on the part of men who have not given one bit of their brain to create what I have written, one cent of their money to help me write what I have written, nor one moment of their time to aid me to write what I have written. This is a straight, brazen, shameless pirate raid that is being made upon me. My back is up against the wall, and I am fighting hard, and I am calling upon you to help me out.

In the past you have bought work of mine and published it in your magazine. You will know the method of copyrighting you pursued at that time without my going into the details of this here.

I am asking you now, to assign to me, and to send to me the document in which you assign, any and all rights, with the exception of first-serial rights in the United States and Canada, in all stories, articles, essays, novels and plays written by me and purchased and published and copyrighted by you between the years and months of years beginning January 1, 1898, and ending October 12, 1913, inclusive.

The portion of the period above inclosed in dates practically covers the days previous to the appearance in the publishing game of second-serial rights, during which time you were publishing my work.

The basis of this request which I am making you in this letter is that when you copyrighted the various numbers of your publication, you did copyright all rights in the contents thereof, and that you did hold in trust for me all other rights except those first-serial rights already described in the foregoing part of this letter.

If you will kindly have a clerk run through your index for the data, and in the assignment you send to me, specify by title and date of publication, it will be of immense assistance to me in this my hour of rush, in which I am writing some eighty-odd periodicals which have published my work serially since I entered the writing game. Also, I beg of you, because of this necessity for haste on my part, that you will forgive the manner and method of this request I am preferring to you.

If you can see your way to it, please help me out by sending me this assignment at your very earliest convenience.

Sincerely yours,

JACK LONDON.

The Real Jack London in Hawaii

By Mae Lacy Baggs

I HAD known Jack London in San Francisco, I had visited the London ranch house at Santa Rosa, but never had I known the real Jack London until I saw him in Hawaii.

Before I had scented in him something of the Wolf Larsen of "The Sea Wolf," cruel, relentless, tyrannical; something of the breeder in his "Little Lady of the Big House," cold, scientific, materialist; but in Hawaii—a land loving and lovely—he was different. I like to think that I know it to be true that this was the real London, that this land had shown him his real self.

It was our first morning in Honolulu, early in the new year of 1915. We had come out from the Moana Hotel at Waikiki for an early morning plunge. I knew that the Londons had one of the adjacent Seaside Hotel cottages, but my delight was great to find Mrs. London already on the beach. Greetings were scarcely over when Mr. London walked out of the water with his surf-board under his arm.

"Aloha!" was his first word, intoned with the true Hawaiian quaver. And then, "You had to come too?"

He referred, of course, to the well known and strong impelling force that sooner or later reaches all lovers of the rare and beautiful, and draws them to Hawaii, maybe for a month's stay, maybe forever. Time and circumstance, not place, decides the length of stay. If it were just place Hawaii would have to spread its shores and take in the whole world.

It was destined that I see much of the Londons, both in Honolulu and on the other islands. Their cottage at Waikiki Beach was not a stone's throw from the lanai (Hawaiian for veranda) of our beach hotel. Hour after hour, while rainbows played their elusive game, now back up through the Moana Valley, now through sifting spray, liquid sunshine, as the Hawaiian has it, of the dreamlike coral sea, a group of congenial spirits sat around a table on the lanai and talked of strange lands, strange seas and stranger peoples.

The Jack London of popular conception had no relation to the man himself. In a measure he was responsible for this misunderstanding. He never tried to cover up the facts of his lowly birth, his lowly struggles for existence, to say nothing of his struggle for recognition as a writer. Instead, his life was one long attempt to convince the world through his pen that the conditions which produced his pitiful beginnings were all wrong.

His method was chiefly to show up every man as a primitive, with primitive passions—brutes. Now a brute, an animal, in other words, he would argue, never strikes except in self-defence; the corporation, organized capital, itself beyond the reach of a blow, strikes deep and crushes the soul of this primitive, which left to itself would not harm a flea.

But Mr. London did not always talk on such deep, headaching topics. His remarks, his observations, his stories, were as light and as frothy as the spray that dashed over the coral reef and broke on the shore at our feet.

He was at his best when telling South Sea tales, sometimes of the petty, mimick kingdoms set up by conquering Polynesians on an atoll, sometimes of a hog of a trader, as he dubbed the usual white man found at out of the way ports of call. But we

The London party at Honolulu, 1915. Mrs. London is standing on the left.

were always subjected to his wife's revision of the stories he set out to tell, yet always between them was perfect trust and understanding.

"Let me see, Jack," she would interpose, a merry twinkle dancing in her eyes, "just—what—story—is—that?"

Without any show of resentment ever, he would come back with a word that would at once act as a cue. As often as not, looking the assembly over, Mrs. London would say:

"No, mate. Tell this one——" starting him off with a keynote.

One night he was particularly eager to go beyond his wife's ruling, and, looking us over, his eyes rested on me, when he said:

"I do wish I knew all of you better —for this is a good story."

It was plain Mr. London's contact with a life that had few frills had made him indifferent to social amenities, to the small conventions that brand a thing too risque, taboo.

You must know that Mr. London had no parlor upbringing and few parlor manners did he acquire. He never got over feeling self-conscious in the presence of some one born into a walk of life commonly considered above his. Never by a word did he recognize class, but his manner betrayed instinctive reverence for that elusive yet unmistakable something known as "breeding."

His greeting always bore that "Pleased to meet you" smile. Somehow his diffidence matched his appearance, matched his shambling gait, his shock or unruly hair, his soft collared shirts, his loose belted, unpressed trousers. For, as to looks, Mr. London was not a lady's man, if we accept the model men writers place to our credit. But Mr. London was a man's man, therefore, a woman's man. More than that, he was a child's man.

Illustrative of the latter trait is the following incident:

On a ranch on Maui, the high island three islands away, as distance is measured in the Hawaiian archipelago, where the Londons had gone when the weather had become too hot for creative work in Honolulu, Mr. London had taken a marked interest at once in the little daughters of his host, Louis von Temsky. The first night after dinner we were sitting on the large lanai overlooking a valley that reached down to the sea. One of the children, a little girl of 9, encouraged by a friendly smile in Mr. London's eyes, sidled up to the writer and said shyly:

"Mr. London, we," indicating her sister of twelve who took herself seriously as an artist and liked to be read to in her garret studio while so employed, "we have been reading one of your books."

In a manner not quite sure of himself and shy as the child's he replied:

"Have you? Which one?"

" 'The Valley of the Moon,' " replied the little girl.

"How far have you read?" Mr. Lon-

don was as hesitant as the little bread and butter girl herself.

With a choke in her throat from holding a conversation with the book's author, the big man himself, she looked helplessly at her sister.

"Oh, sister—where were we reading yesterday—when we got so sleepy?"

For a moment the air was tense; then Mrs. London, who is graciousness itself, broke the spell with a ringing laugh.

"There, mate," she crowed, "I hope that will hold you for a while."

The little maiden blanched, not sure just what she had done, but Mr. London was the first to her assistance. His big heart dominated the moment and presently they were deep in child stuff.

Of Jack London's relation with his wife, Charmian, he always called her, it hurts me to talk, now that he is gone. Always she was his "mate." They were constantly together—more so in Hawaii than elsewhere, for his interests on the ranch or his big holdings down in the Imperial Valley of Southern California called him far afield. In Hawaii it was different. Even while her husband was writing his thousand words a day, his "bit," he called it, she was always hovering near, ready at a word to do his bidding.

Mr. London's Japanese secretary, who typed his "stuff"—Mr. London always wrote in long hand—on a small aluminum typewriter, married a pretty little Japanese maiden while in Honolulu. The Londons' treatment of the pair was beautiful to see. They accorded them all the forms and ceremonies of the Nipponese in addition to American ways.

Mr. London first visited the Hawaiian Islands when on his projected world tour with the Snark. Unfortunately, for a while at least, the people of Hawaii felt rather unkind toward the writer because of the writeup he gave the leper colony on Molokai. Later, however, they recognized that his criticism had been most friendly and provocative of good results, and no man has ever set foot on those most

Jack London in swimming rig to ride the huge beach combers with the
natives at Honolulu.

hospitable shores who has received, in the years since, such a warm, wet welcome as that accorded Jack London.

Last year, when the committee appointed by Congress to investigate the sugar conditions in the islands was being entertained, it was to Jack London that the Hawaiian Promotion Club looked for first aid in showing visitors the real charms and wonders of the islands. He had a free hand, and was told to stop at no length in the way of entertainment. And he didn't.

But like another master mind he

could save others from being denied their wants, himself he could not save. It was up at the Volcano House, the hotel that sits at the edge of Kilauea's crater. Well, it was a hot day. And the Congressmen, surely to a man, had been thirsty. Julian Monsarrat, manager of the Kapapala ranch, felt himself suddenly pulled by the coat tails.

"I say, Julian, the Scotch is all gone. Er—is there—any down at your ranch?"

"Sure!" And Mr. Monsarrat called to his Jap driver, who was gazing at the spewing sulphur beds. "Just look up Wang, he has the keys to the cellarette!" he sang out after the disappearing car.

A few weeks later we were guests at the ranch. Mr. Monsarrat told us the story.

It seems Wang, the Chinese butler, was not in sight when the ranch house was reached, and of course Mr. London could not lose any time looking for keys. The handsome koa wood door was splintered. I think he must have used a meat axe. But Mr. Monsarrat only fondled the door to his cellarette lovingly and laughed at "Jack's playfulness."

And Jack was playful. The act of wilfully, willingly destroying a handsome piece of property seems incongruous to us, but to him it was simply a good joke on his friend. We have to take into account his untamed nature. He probably didn't stop to reflect upon his act, but it was at once his interpretation of life—a rebellion against standards and established order.

Along the Oakland waterfront the old salts will now be recounting ripping tales of the "young daredevil London" who could drink any man down at the bar, and knock any two of then down at once who had the temerity to refuse his invitation to "line up." Yet it is difficult to think of such colossal strength as ascribed to him.

For Mr. London was barely of average height. True, his shoulders were a bit more than medium broad, but his chest was far from a full one. And then there was a looseness about his frame that kept down the suggestion of strength or physical prowess.

He was probably underfed as a lad, and his early dissipation, which he tells of without hesitation in his "John Barleycorn," which is largely autobiographical—he bought beer instead of peanuts—accounts for his failure to fill out later. Then, too, no man or boy who ships before the mast on a wind-jammer or its equivalent in the guise of a deckhand is going to have half enough sleep, much less enough hard-tack. If they did, they'd get lazy, the rascals, an old salt would tell you, and unfit for work.

Now, Mr. London may have lived —but his face and his figure told in their lines of deprivation and struggle that the after years of plenty could not erase what the effort of making each phase of life give its secret had cost him.

No doubt the reason Hawaii appealed to him so intensely was because here life was virtually without effort. Back on the ranch were the tremendous breeding problems his anthropological mind had set as his task; down on his vast holdings in the Imperial valley was being tried out plant breeding and cross breeding, but here in Hawaii, which he was beginning to call his real home, he warmed to the suggestion of ease that each zephyr whispered.

To him the lull of the swishing sea was a new language, and the whole of the islands spoke of a life he had failed to grasp, the joys really to be found in a dolce far niente existence. "All that beauty, all that wealth e'er gave" was here within reach. And there was more still.

There was the Hawaiian aloha. Hawaiian love. Not only is this beautiful spirit of love found in the natives, but each man, woman and child, haole, malihini or kamaaina, even though he has it not upon arrival, finds it soon sinking into his soul

And Jack London early breathed it out.

And they'll miss him in Hawaii.

And they'll pay his memory respect with a memorial service in the native church, and wave high huge black feather kahilis on a staff back and forth to the recurrent beat of the ancient song of the native wailers. And then there will follow stories of London, stories of his kindness and attention to scores of their number, for his face and ambling gait had become as familiar to them as one of their kind.

Fishers by the sea, with spear poised, stopped their spear in midair to sing out "alohas" to his call from a neighbor crag; ofttimes in the same spirit was he welcomed by the waders on the beach at night who flashed a torch to attract the finny tribe. Like them too he wore sandals with wooden heels and toe pieces to save the bare feet from the coral pebbles in the shallow waters. From the native, too, he had learned to manage a surfboat as skillfully as any Kanaka, a thing possible to only a strangely privileged few who have not grown up in the "strange South Seas."

It is difficult to tell just when Mr. London did the quantity of writing that came from his pen. He was so much in evidence in Honolulu and elsewhere in the islands that it seemed hardly possible to associate him with the prolific writer he was known to be. A novel of his, "Jerry," a dog story, announced to begin as a serial in one of the magazines next month, was finished in Honolulu early in 1915, while another dog novel to be called "Michael" (each of about 80,000 words) was about completed when he and Mrs. London sailed for San Francisco in July of that year.

They returned to the islands in January following, and in a high powered Jap sampan made a trip to the outlying islands and as far as Midway. Only recently—in early August, in fact—the press reported that Mr. and Mrs. London had again returned from their new love, Hawaii, that Mr. London might be present at the Bohemian Club's annual outing, its High Jinks.

For years Mr. London has been its guiding spirit, and although celebrities belong to this unique organization and come from all over the world to attend its annual outing, there was none whose laugh was listened for as was London's. From the night of the Low Jinks, when the ceremony of "cremating care" takes place, until a week later, when the Grove play ushers in the High Jinks, this man who had the spirit of boy eternal in him, played pranks and practical jokes on the unsuspecting. The same press report, said the Londons would again return to Honolulu after the first of the new year.

How little one knows of what fate holds in store is shown in some advice Mr. London gave to young writers a few years ago. He spoke of his first acceptance.

He had built up his case cleverly as to his willingness to accept the minimum rate, which by some form of reasoning his unseasoned experience had told was $40. And the check was for $5. To quote: "That I did not die then and there convinces me that I am possessed of a singular ruggedness of soul which will permit me to qualify for the oldest inhabitant."

And had it been possible to purchase a lease on mortal lift by "ruggedness of soul," succeeding generations would have known—and also loved—Mr. London in his Hawaiian home. But it was not to be.

Yet to Hawaii there has fallen a lot drawn by four places, to be chosen from all the world—for Mr. London had traveled far—as the preferred home of a man of such unusual character and ability. What Stevenson was to Samoa, London was to Hawaii, and more. Hawaii is come more and more to the public eye; it is more in the beaten path. It will have those who come after who would sing its paeans of praise. But the "aloha" of the Hawaiian is a faithful one. Just as Mr. London's last few stories were headed "My Hawaiian Aloha," so will Mr. London be the Hawaiian's aloha, last and best.

Jack London and his prize stallion Neuadd Hillside. The horse died some two weeks before his master.

Valley of the Moon Ranch

A Recent Visit There

By Bailey Millard

EVEN the pig-pens on Jack London's ranch are models of solidity, service and sanitation, his two enormous silos are towers of concrete strength, his stables are good examples of stability, his corrals are high and strong, and his livestock is the finest, the sleekest and the most high-bred and altogether desirable to be found in all Sonoma County. Indeed, some of his horses are famed throughout the nation and have taken Exposition and State Fair honors.

Jack London's ranch is near Glen Ellen, in Sonoma County, Cal., and most of it is on gently sloping hillsides that were formerly covered with vines and fruit trees. Mr. London has grubbed up most of the vines, not for Prohibitionist, but for utilitarian reasons. The old winehouses, most of them built many years ago by Kohler & Frohling, are now occupied as stables, shops and sheds, and one of them, near the London residence, is used as a dining room.

There are over 1,300 acres in the ranch, which includes five or six smaller holding, among them being one of the very first commercial vineyards in California.

Literature and livestock seem a happy combination when viewed from the front veranda of the London home. Inside, one may see the author of "The Valley of the Moon" writing a story, and outside may be seen the pleasant terraces where he or rather his men have written even more largely and legibly with plow and cultivator. For the farmer, after all, whether he sells stories to publishers or keeps them in his own head, has written bigger things than the magazinist, bigger indeed than Dante or Milton. The work of the mere literat may not be in the least nutritious to body or soul, but there is not the slightest doubt as to the food value of the farmer's product.

"I call this place 'The Ranch of Good Intentions," said Mr. London to me, as we went over the smooth roads in an automobile that probably represented the price of a single short story, written in three or four days. No, Mr. London was not at the wheel. The best of cars is not of as much attraction to him as a good riding horse, and the highland trail is more pleasing than the smoothest of State highways. "At first my ranching was more or less of a joke, but it has turned to earnest at last. When I first came here, tired of cities and city people, I settled down on a little farm over there in what is now a corner of my holding. The land was all worn out from years and years of unintelligent farming, as is this whole ranch for that matter, and I didn't attempt to raise much of anything. All I wanted was a quiet place in the country to write and loaf in, and to get out of Nature that something which we all need, only the most of us don't know it.

"I liked those hills up there. They were beautiful, as you see, and I wanted beauty. So I extended the boundary up to the top of that ridge and all along it. In order to do that I had to buy a big piece of this lower land, for the watershed went with the valley estates, and was hardly separable from them. That is the reason why I now have over two sections of land, but it all plays into my game, which is beauty first and livestock second. There's plenty of fine grazing land up there on that ridge, and along the sides of the canyon, and if the season hadn't been such a dry one you would see a pretty little stream running down that way." He pointed up through a green rift of the hills. There were tall, straight redwoods there, and firs, live oaks, madrones, manzanitas and laurels.

"I bought beauty," he went on, "and with beauty I was content for awhile. It pleases me more than anything else now, but I am putting this ranch into first-class shape and am laying a foundation for a good paying industry here.

"Everything I build is for the years to come. Those walls you see along this road ought to last a long time, don't you think?"

The walls were certainly solid looking and strong enough, being constructed of good hard rock, quarried on the ranch. Men were at work in the fields removing the nigger-heads and piling them along the fences. Much of this field rock is used in building foundations for water troughs and tanks, the basins of which are of solid concrete which put to shame the old wooden affairs used by most of the Sonoma Valley farmers.

"I designed those hog houses and pens myself," said the author proudly. There was a round central structure of rock and cement with a peaked concrete roof, surrounded by sheds of the same material. When the Childe Roland pig comes to that round tower he gets a good square meal of ground alfalfa and grain, for it is the feed house, down from the upper story of which the feed pours automatically through square galvanized iron leaders

The famous concrete palatial quarters of the high-bred porkers.

into a cement basin, where it is mixed with water from a big pipe and is then conveyed out to the surrounding troughs, where the Duroc Jerseys munch and grunt contentedly. The hog pens all have concrete floors, but the hogs lie upon movable wooden planks at night. The pens are ranged all around the central tower, which stands in the inclosure made by them. There are corrals surounding the whole place, which is well shaded by oaks and madrones.

Everything in the hog department is spick and span, as the hose is played upon the floors, cleansing them at regular intervals and making them cleaner than the floors of many a squalid ranch house I have seen elsewhere.

Ah, and do you think to enter this hog swine sanctuary without becoming genuflections and prostrations! Well, at least, before you pass the gate you must step aside into a little pagoda and rub your feet upon the prayer rug. On that rug is a sticky carbolized mixture to disinfect your feet, so that your profane, microbe-laden shoes shall not carry to that precious, cleanly band any germs of cholera. Never but once has the dread disease been borne within the inclosure, and that was when somebody walked upon a butcher's floor and then into the pens. But now cholera is unknown among the London swine.

"I am not raising livestock for the butcher," said Mr. London, "but for the breeder or anybody who wants the best of thoroughbreds. Of course, the culls will be killed, but my idea is not to raise anything here that can't be driven out on hoof."

Mrs. Elizabeth Shepard, who is the manager of the ranch, showed me the horses and cattle. Among them are many prize winners. Neuadd Hillside, a $25,000 English shire stallion, is among the most imposing of the bunch. He won the grand championship at the State fair in 1912, and with other London horses and mares picked up most of the horse prizes at the recent Santa Rosa fair. Another beautiful stallion is Mountain Lad, named for the horse hero in "The Little Lady of the Big House." Beside there are five brood mares and four wonderful colts coming on. The grade horses include seven work teams, which are kept busy most of the time. Mrs. London takes great interest in the horses, and is a fine rider.

The cattle include some beautiful Jersey cows and one magnificent bull.

Mrs. Shepard is sure of further honors for her equine and bovine charges at the coming Sacramento Fair.

Fifty-five Angora goats and 600 White Leghorn fowls, with a flock of beautiful pheasants, go to make up the rest of the stock and poultry.

Mr. London employs some of the best horsemen to be found anywhere, among them being Hazen Cowan, who won the world's championship for handling bucking horses at the San Jose round-up, and Thomas Harrison, who not only knows horses, but is an expert cattleman.

A feature of the ranch is the big eucalyptus grove, now three years old. Mr. London is raising 65,000 of these trees for hardwood lumber.

Although he knows far more about literature than he does about farming, Mr. London has learned many things from his agricultural experience. On the hillsides his contours are fine examples of how to retain moisture upon sloping land. He believes in fertilizing by tillage and has gotten excellent results by plowing in rye and vetch. He has studied soil innoculation by legumes and other means, and next year he expects to reap some famous crops of barley, hay, alfalfa and corn.

"It is all very interesting," he told me, "and has a literary value to me. Wherever I travel, when I see any growing crop, it means something to me now, though it never did before. Yes, I am a believer in the spineless cactus as animal food, and have set out quite a patch of it. Those who contend that cactus, being 90 per cent water, is of no food value to stock, should go down to Hawaii, where some of the finest, fattest cattle in the world live on cactus that is covered with spines in the unproductive months, getting both food and water from it."

The Ranch of Good Intentions has been cultivated by its present proprietor only three years, and in a really effective way, for only a year or two, so that, of course, it is not on a paying basis at present, but the intelligent and really scientific methods now employed there are bound to make it profitable in time. Among his products this season are ten tons of prunes.

The Son of the Wolf

By Jack London

(Like all young and untried authors, Jack London spent laborious years in preparing stories for the regular monthlies and weeklies throughout the country, without attracting any attention. In the latter part of 1898, the then editor of Overland Monthly accepted the first of five stories, The Malemute Kid series, all dealing with Jack London's recent experiences in Alaska. The tales readily illustrate the vivid art of story telling which the author was rapidly acquiring. He had found himself. The Malemute Kid stories attracted wide attention and a little later London found no difficulty in placing his stories with eastern publications. Before the close of that year London was well on his successful career. The following story, "The Son of the Wolf" is the third of "The Malemute Kid" series.)

MAN rarely places a proper valuation upon his womankind, at least not until deprived of them. He has no conception of the subtle atmosphere exhaled by the sex feminine, so long as he bathes in it; but let it be withdrawn, and an evergrowing void begins to manifest itself in his existence, and he becomes hungry, in a vague sort of way, for a something so indefinite that he cannot characterize it. If his comrades have no more experience than himself, they will shake their heads dubiously and dose him with strong physic. But the hunger will continue and become stronger; he will lose interest in the things of his every-day life and wax morbid; and one day, when the emptiness has become unbearable, a revelation will dawn upon him.

In the Yukon country, when this comes to pass, the man usually provisions a poling-boat, if it is summer, and if winter, harnesses his dogs, and heads for the Southland. A few months later, supposing him to be possessed of a faith in the country, he returns with a wife to share with him in that faith, and incidentally in his hardships. This but serves to show the innate selfishness of man. It also brings us to the trouble of "Scruff" Mackenzie, which occurred in the old days, before the country was stampeded and staked by a tidal-wave of che-cha-quas, and when the Klondike's only claim to notice was its salmon fisheries.

"Scruff" Mackenzie bore the earmarks of a frontier birth and a frontier life. His face was stamped with twenty-five years of incessant struggle with Nature in her wildest moods—the last two the wildest and hardest of all, having been spent in groping for the gold which lies in the shadow of the Arctic Circle. When the yearning sickness came upon him, he was not surprised, for he was a practical man and had seen other men thus stricken. But he showed no sign of his malady, save that he worked harder. All summer he fought mosquitoes and washed for the sure-thing bars of the Stuart River for a double grub-stake. Then he floated a raft of house logs down the Yukon to Forty Mile, and put together as comfortable a cabin as any the camp could boast of. In fact, it showed such cozy promise that many men elected to be his partner and to come and live with him. But he crushed their aspirations with rough speech, peculiar for its strength and brevity, and bought a double supply of grub from the trading post.

As has been noted, "Scruff" Mackenzie was a practical man. If he wanted a thing he usually got it, but in doing so, went no farther out of his way than was necessary. Though a son of toil and hardship, he was averse to a journey of six hundred miles on the ice, a second of two thousand miles on the ocean, and still a third thousand miles or so to his last stamping-grounds—all in the mere quest of a wife. Life was too short. So he rounded up his dogs, lashed a curious freight to his sled, and faced across the divide whose westward slopes were drained by the head-reaches of the Tanana.

He was a sturdy traveler, and his

wolf-dogs could work harder and travel farther on less grub than any other team in the Yukon. Three weeks later he strode into a hunting-camp of the Upper Tanana Sticks. They marveled at his temerity; for they had a bad name and had been known to kill white men for as trifling a thing as a sharp ax or a broken rifle. But he went among them single-handed, his bearing being a delicious composite of humility, familiarity, sang-froid, and insolence. It required a deft hand and deep knowledge of the barbaric mind effectually to handle such diverse weapons; but he was a past-master in the art, knowing when to conciliate and when to threaten with Jove-like wrath.

He first made obeisance to the Chief Thling-Tinneh, presenting him with a couple of pounds of black tea and tobacco, and thereby winning his most cordial regard. Then he mingled with the men and maidens, and that night gave a pot-lach. The snow was beaten down in the form of an oblong, perhaps a hundred feet in length, and quarter as many across. Down the center a long fire was built, while either side was carpeted with spruce boughs. The lodges were forsaken, and the fivescore or so members of the tribe gave tongue to their folk-chants in honor of their guest.

"Scruff" Mackenzie's two years had taught him the not many hundred words of their vocabulary, and he had likewise conquered their deep gutturals, their Japanese idioms, constructions and honorific and agglutinative particles. So he made oration after their manner, satisfying their instinctive poetry-love with crude flights of eloquence and metaphorical contortions. After Thling-Tinneh and the Shaman had responded in kind, he made trifling presents to the menfolk, joined in their singing, and proved an expert in their fifty-two-stick gambling game.

And they smoked his tobacco and were pleased. But among the younger men there was a defiant attitude, a spirit of braggadocio, easily understood by the raw insinuations of the toothless squaws and the giggling of the maidens. They had known few white men, "Sons of the Wolf," but from those few they had learned strange lessons.

Nor had "Scruff" Mackenzie, for all his seeming carelessness, failed to note these phenomena. In truth, rolled in his sleeping-furs, he thought it all over, thought seriously, and emptied many pipes in mapping out a campaign. One maiden only had caught his fancy—none other than Zarinska, daughter to the chief. In features, form and poise, answering more nearly to the white man's type of beauty, she was almost an anomaly among her tribal sisters. He would possess her, make her his wife, and name her—ah, he would name her Gertrude! Having thus decided, he rolled over on his side and dropped off to sleep, a true son of his all-conquering race, a Samson among the Philistines.

It was slow work and a stiff game; but "Scruff" Mackenzie maneuvered cunningly, with an unconcern which served to puzzle the Sticks. He took great care to impress the man that he was a sure shot and a mighty hunter, and the camp rang with his plaudits when he brought down a moose at six hundred yards. Of a night he visited in Chief Thling-Tinneh's lodge of moose and caribou skins, talking big and dispensing tobacco with a lavish hand. Nor did he fail to likewise honor the Shaman; for he realized the medicine-man's influence, with his people, and was anxious to make of him an ally. But that worthy was high and mighty, refused to be propitiated, and was unerringly marked down as a prospective enemy.

Though no opening presented for an interview with Zarinska, Mackenzie stole many a glance at her, giving fair warning of his intent. And well she knew, yet coquettishly surrounded herself with a ring of women whenever the men were away, and he had a chance. But he was in no hurry; besides, he knew she could not help but think of him, and a few days of such thought would only better his suit.

At last, one night, when he deemed the time to be ripe, he abruptly left the chief's smoky dwelling and hastened to a neighboring lodge. As usual, she sat with squaws and maidens about her, all engaged in sewing moccasins and beadwork. They laughed at his entrance, and badinage, which linked Zarinska to him, ran high. But one after the other they were unceremoniously bundled into the outer snow, whence they hurried to spread the tale through all the camp.

His cause was well pleaded, in her tongue, for she did not know his, and at the end of two hours he rose to go.

"So Zarinska will come to the White Man's lodge? Good! I go now to have talk with thy father, for he may not be so minded. And I will give him many tokens; but he must not ask too much. If he say no? Good! Zarinska shall yet come to the White Man's lodge."

He had already lifted the skin flap to depart, when a low exclamation brought him back to the girl's side. She brought herself to her knees on the bearskin mat, her face aglow with true Eve-light, and shyly unbuckled his heavy belt. He looked down, perplexed, suspicious, his ears alert for the slightest sound without. But her next move disarmed his doubt, and he smiled with pleasure. She took from her sewing bag a moosehide sheath, brave with bright beadwork, fantastically designed. She drew his great hunting-knife gazed reverently along the keen edge, half tempted to try it with her thumb, and shot it into place in its new home. Then she slipped the sheath along the belt to its customary resting-place, just above the hip.

For all the world, it was like a scene of olden time—a lady and her knight. Mackenzie drew her up full height and swept her red lips with his moustache—the, to her, foreign caress of the Wolf. It was a meeting of the stone age and the steel; but she was none the less a woman, as her crimson cheek and the luminous softness of her eyes attested.

There was a thrill of excitement in the air as "Scruff" Mackenzie, a bulky bundle under his arm, threw open the flap of Thling-Tinneh's tent. Children were running about in the open, dragging dry wood to the scene of the potlach, a babble of women's voices was growing in intensity, the young men were consulting in sullen groups, while from the Shaman's lodge rose the eerie sounds of an incantation.

The chief was alone with his blear-eyed wife, but a glance sufficed to tell Mackenzie that the news was already old. So he plunged at once into the business, shifting the beaded sheath prominently to the fore as advertisement of the betrothal.

"O Thling-Tinneh, mighty chief of the Sticks and the land of the Tanana, ruler of the salmon and the bear, the moose and the caribou! The White Man is before thee with a great purpose. Many moons has his lodge been empty, and he is lonely. And his heart has eaten itself in silence, and grown hungry for a woman to sit beside him in his lodge, to meet him from the hunt with warm fire, and good food. He has heard strange things, the patter of baby moccasins and the sound of children's voices. And one night a vision came upon him, and he beheld the Raven, who is thy father, the great Raven, who is the father of all the Sticks. And the Raven spake to the lonely White Man, saying: 'Bind thou thy moccasins upon thee, and gird thy snow-shoes on, and lash thy sled with food for many sleeps and fine tokens for the Chief Thling-Tinneh. For thou shalt turn thy face to where the mid-spring sun is wont to sink below the land and journey to this great chief's hunting-grounds. There thou shalt make big presents, and Thling-Tinneh, who is my son, shall become to thee as a father. In his lodge there is a maiden into whom I breathed the breath of life for thee. This maiden shalt thou take to wife.'

"O Chief, thus spake the great Raven; thus do I lay many presents at thy feet; thus am I come to take thy daughter!"

The old man drew his furs about him with crude consciousness of royalty, but delayed reply while a youngster crept in, delivered a quick message to appear before the council, and was gone.

"O White Man, whom we have named Moose-killer, also known as the Wolf, and the Son of the Wolf! We know thou comest of a mighty race; we are proud to have thee our potlach guest; but the king-salmon does not mate with the dog-salmon, nor the Raven with the Wolf."

"Not so!" cried Mackenzie. "The daughters of the Raven have I met in the camps of the Wolf—the squaw of Mortimer, the squaw of Tregidgo, the squaw of Barnaby, who came two ice-runs back, and I have heard of other squaws, though my eyes beheld them not."

"Son, your words are true; but it were evil mating, like the water with the sand, like the snow-flake with the sun. But met you one Mason and his squaw? No? He came ten ice-runs ago—the first of all the Wolves. And with him there was a mighty man, straight as a willow-shoot, and tall; strong as the bald-faced grizzly, with a heart like the full-summer moon; his——"

"Oh!" interrupted Mackenzie, recognizing the well known Northland figure—"Malemute Kid!"

"The same—a mighty man. But saw you aught of the squaw? She was full sister to Zarinska!"

"Nay, Chief; but I have heard. Mason—far, far to the north, a spruce-tree, heavy with years, crushed out his life beneath. But his love was great, and he had much gold. With this, and her boy, she journeyed countless sleeps toward the winter's noonday sun, and there she yet lives—no biting frost, no snow, no summer's midnight sun, no winter's noonday night."

A second messenger interrupted with imperative summons from the council. As Mackenzie threw him into the snow, he caught a glimpse of the swaying forms before the council-fire, heard the deep basses of the man in rhythmic chant, and knew the Shaman was fanning the anger of his people. Time pressed. He turned upon the chief.

"Come! I wish thy child. And now, see! Here are tobacco, tea, many cups of sugar, warm blankets, handkerchiefs, both good and large; and here, a true rifle, with many bullets and much powder."

"Nay," replied the old man, struggling against the great wealth spread before him. "Even now are my people come together. They will not have this marriage."

"But thou art chief!"

"Yet do my young men rage because the Wolves have taken their maidens so that they may not marry."

"Listen, O Thling-Tinneh! Ere the night has passed into the day, the Wolf shall face his dogs to the Mountains of the East and fare forth to the Country of the Yukon. And Zarinska shall break trail for his dogs."

"And ere the night has gained its middle, my young men may fling to the dogs the flesh of the Wolf, and his bones be scattered in the snow till the springtime lays them bare."

It was threat and counter-threat. Mackenzie's bronzed face flushed darkly. He raised his voice. The old squaw, who till now had sat an impassive spectator, made to creep by him for the door. The song of the men broke suddenly and there was a hubbub of many voices as he whirled the old woman roughly to her couch of skins.

"Again I cry—listen, O Thling-Tenneh! The Wolf dies with teeth fast-locked, and with him there shall sleep ten of thy strongest men—men who are needed, for the hunting is but begun, and the fishing is not many moons away. And again, of what profit should I die? I know the custom of thy people; thy share of my wealth shall be very small. Grant me thy child, and it shall be all thine. And yet again, my brothers will come, and they are many, and their maws are never filled; and the daughters of the Raven shall bear children in the lodges of the Wolf. My people are greater than thy people. It is destiny. Grant, and all this wealth is thine!"

Moccasins were crunching the snow without. Mackenzie threw his rifle to cock, and loosened the twin Colts in his belt.

"Grant, O Chief!"

"And yet will my people say no."

"Grant, and the wealth is thine. Then shall I deal with thy people after."

"The Wolf will have it so. I will take his tokens—but I would warn him."

Mackenzie passed over the goods, taking care to clog the rifle's ejector, and capping the bargain with a kaleidoscopic silk kerchief. The Shaman and half a dozen young braves entered, but he shouldered boldly among them and passed out.

"Pack!" was his laconic greeting to Zarinska as he passed her lodge and hurried to harness his dogs. A few minutes later he swept into the council at the head of the team, the woman by his side. He took his place at the upper end of the oblong, by the side of the chief. To his left, a step to the rear, he stationed Zarinska—her proper place. Besides, the time was ripe for mischief, and there was need to guard his back.

On either side, the men crouched to the fire, their voices lifted in a folkchant out of the forgotten past. Full of strange, halting cadences and haunting recurrences, it was not beautiful. "Fearful" may inadequately express it. At the lower end, under the eye of the Shaman, danced half a score of women. Stern were his reproofs to those who did not wholly abandon themselves to the ecstasy of the rite. Half hidden in their heavy masses of raven hair, all dishevelled and falling to their waists, they slowly swayed to and fro, their forms rippling to an ever-changing rhythm.

It was a weird scene; an anachronism. To the south, the nineteenth century was reeling off the few years of its last decade; here flourished man primeval, a shade removed from the prehistoric cave-dweller, a forgotten fragment of the Elder World. The tawny wolf-dogs sat between their skin clad masters or fought for room, the firelight cast backward from their red eyes and dripping fangs. The woods, in ghostly shroud, slept on unheeding. The White Silence, for the moment driven to the rimming forest, seemed ever crushing inward; the stars danced with great leaps, as is their wont in the time of the Great Cold; while the Spirits of the Pole trailed their robes of glory athwart the heavens.

"Scruff" Mackenzie dimly realized the wild grandeur of the setting as his eyes ranged down the fur-fringed sides in quest of missing faces. They rested for a moment on a new-born babe, suckling at its mother's naked breast. It was forty below—seventy and odd degrees of frost. He thought of the tender women of his own race and smiled grimly. Yet from the loins of some such tender woman had he sprung with a kingly inheritance—an inheritance which gave to him and his dominance over the land and sea, over the animals and the peoples of all the zones. Single-handed against fivescore, girt by the Arctic winter, far from his own, he felt the promptings of his heritage, the desire to possess, the wild danger-love, the thrill of battle, the power to conquer or to die.

The singing and the dancing ceased, and the Shaman flared up in rude eloquence. Through the sinuosities of their vast mythology, he worked cunningly upon the credulity of his people. The case was strong. Opposing the creative principles as embodied in the Crow and the Raven, he stigmatized Mackenzie as the Wolf, the fighting and destructive principle. Not only was the combat of these forces spiritual, but men fought, each to his totem. They were the children of Jelchs, the Raven, the Promethéan fire bringer; Mackenzie was the child of the Wolf, or in other words, the Devil. For them to bring a truce to this perpetual warfare, to marry their daughters to the arch enemy, were treason and blasphemy of the highest order. No phrase was harsh nor figure vile enough in branding Mackenzie as a sneaking interloper and emissary of Satan. There was a subdued, savage roar in the deep chests of his listeners as he took the swing of his peroration.

"Aye, my brothers, Jelchs is all-powerful! Did he not bring heaven-born fire that we might be warm? Did he not draw the sun, moon and stars from their holes that we might see? Did he not teach us that we might fight the Spirits of Famine and of Frost? But now Jelchs is angry with his children, and they are grown to a handful, and he will not help. For they have forgotten him, and done evil things, and trod bad trails, and taken his enemies into their lodges to sit by their fires. And the Raven is sorrowful at the wickedness of his children; but when they shall rise up and show they have come back, he will come out of the darkness to aid them. O brothers! the Fire-Bringer has whispered messages to thy Shaman; the same shall ye hear. Let the young men take the young women to their lodges; let them fly at the throat of the Wolf; let them be undying in their enmity! Then shall their women become fruitful and they shall multiply into a mighty people! And the Raven shall lead great tribes of their fathers and their fathers' fathers from out of the North; and they shall beat back the Wolves till they are as last year's camp fires; and they shall again come to rule over all the land! 'Tis the message of Jelchs, the Raven."

This foreshadowing of the Messiah's coming brought a hoarse howl from the Sticks as they leaped to their feet.

Mackenzie slipped the thumbs of his mittens and waited. There was a clamor for the "Fox," not to be stilled till one of the young men stepped forward to speak.

"Brothers! The Shaman has spoken wisely. The Wolves have taken our women and our men are childless. We are grown to a handful. The Wolves have taken our warm furs and given for them evil spirits which dwell in bottles, and clothes which come not from the beaver or the lynx, but are made from the grass. And they are not warm, and our men die of strange sicknesses. I, the Fox, have taken no woman to wife; and why? Twice have the maidens which pleased me gone to the camps of the Wolf. Even now have I laid by skins of the beaver, of the moose, of the caribou that I might win favor in the eyes of Thling-Tinneh that I might wed Zarinska, his daughter. Even now are her snow shoes bound to her feet, ready to break trail for the dogs of the Wolf. Nor do I speak for myself alone. As I have done, so has the Bear. He, too, had fain been the father of her children, and many skins has he cured thereto. I speak for all the young men who know not wives. The Wolves are ever hungry. Always do they take the choice meat at the killing. To the Ravens are left the leavings.

"There is Gugkla," he cried, brutally pointing out one of the women, who was a cripple. "Her legs are bent like the ribs of a birch canoe. She cannot gather wood nor carry the meat of the hunters. Did the Wolves choose her?"

"Ai! ai!" vociferated his tribesmen.

"There is Moyri, whose eyes are crossed by the Evil Spirit. Even the babes are affrighted when they gaze upon her, and it is said the bald-face gives her the trail. Was she chosen?"

Again the cruel applause rang out.

"And there sits Pischet. She does not hearken to my words. Never has she heard the cry of the chit-chat, the voice of her husband, the babble of her child. She lives in the White Silence. Cared the Wolves aught for her? No! Theirs is the choice of the kill; ours is the leavings.

"Brothers, it shall not be! No more shall the Wolves slink among our camp-fires. The time is come."

A great streamer of fire, the aurora borealis, purple, green and yellow, shot across the zenith, bridging horizon to horizon. With head thrown back and arms extended, he swayed to his climax.

"Behold! The spirits of our fathers have arisen, and great deeds are afoot this night."

He stepped back, and another young man somewhat diffidently came forward, pushed on by his comrades. He towered a full head above them, his broad chest defiantly bared to the frost. He swung tentatively from one foot to the other. Words halted upon his tongue, and he was ill at ease. His face was horrible to look upon, for it had at one time been half torn away by some terrific blow. At last he struck his breast with his clenched fist, drawing sound as from a drum, and his voice rumbled forth as does the surf from an ocean cavern.

"I am the Bear—the Silver-Tip and the Son of the Silver-Tip! When my voice was yet as a girl's, I slew the lynx, the moose and the caribou; when it whistled like the wolverines from under a cache, I crossed the Mountains of the South and slew three of the White Rivers; when it became as the roar of the Chinook, I met the bald-faced grizzly, but gave no trail."

At this he paused, his hand significantly sweeping across his hideous scars.

"I am not as the Fox. My tongue is frozen like the river. I cannot make great talk. My words are few. The Fox says great deeds are afoot this night. Good! Talk flows from his tongue like the freshets of the spring, but he is chary of deeds. This night shall I do battle with the Wolf. I shall slay him, and Zarinska shall sit by my fire. The Bear has spoken."

Though pandemonium raged about him, "Scruff" Mackenzie held his ground. Aware how useless was the rifle at close quarters, he slipped both holsters to the fore, ready for action, and drew his mittens till his hands were barely shielded by the elbow gauntlets. He knew there was no hope in attack en masse, but true to his boast, was prepared to die with teeth fast-locked. But the Bear restrained his comrades, beating back the more impetuous with his terrible fist. As the tumult began to die away Mackenzie shot a glance in the direction of Zarinska. It was a superb picture. She was leaning forward on her snow-shoes, lips apart and nostrils quivered, like a tigress about to spring. Her great black eyes were fixed upon her tribesmen, in fear and in defiance. So extreme the tension, she had forgotten to breathe. With one hand pressed spasmodically against her breast and the other as tightly gripped about the dog-whip, she was as turned to stone. Even as he looked, relief came to her. Her muscles loosened; with a heavy sigh she settled back, giving him a look of more than love—of worship.

Thling-Tinneh was trying to speak, but his people drowned his voice. Then Mackenzie strode forward. The Fox opened his mouth to a piercing yell but so savagely did Mackenzie whirl upon him that he shrank back, his larynx all a-gurgle with suppressed sound. His discomfiture was greeted with roars of laughter, and served to soothe his fellows to a listening mood.

"Brothers! The White Man, whom ye have chosen to call the Wolf, came among you with fair words. He was not like the Innuit; he spoke not lies. He came as a friend, as one who would be a brother. But your men have had their say, and the time for soft words is past. First, I will tell you that the Shaman has an evil tongue and is a false prophet, that the messages he spake are not those of the Fire-Bringer. His ears are locked to the voice of the Raven, and out of his own head he weaves cunning fancies, and he has made fools of you. He has no power. When the dogs were killed and eaten and your stomachs were heavy with untanned hide and strips of moccasins; when the old men died, and the old women died, and the babes at the dry dugs of the mothers died; when the land was dark, and ye perished as do the salmon in the fall; aye, when the famine was upon you, did the Shaman bring reward to your hunters? did the Shaman put meat in your bellies? Again I say, the Shaman is without power. Thus I spit upon his face!"

Though taken aback by the sacrilege, there was no uproar. Some of the women were even frightened, but among the men there was an uplifting, as though in preparation or anticipation of the miracle. All eyes were turned upon the two central figures. The priest realized the crucial moment, felt his power tottering, opened his mouth in denunciation, but fled backward before the truculent advance, upraised fist and flashing eyes of Mackenzie. He sneered and resumed:

"Was I stricken dead? Did the lightning burn me? Did the stars fall from the sky and crush me? Pish! I have done with the dog. Now will I tell you of my people, who are the mightiest of all the peoples, who rule in all the lands. At first we hunt as I hunt, alone. After that we hunt in packs; and at last, like the caribou-run, we sweep across all the land. Those whom we take into our lodges live; those who will not come die. Zarinska is a comely maiden, full and strong, fit to become the mother of Wolves. Though I die, such shall she become; for my brothers are many, and they will follow the scent of my dogs. Listen to the Law of the Wolf: "Whoso taketh the life of one Wolf, the forfeit shall ten of his people pay." In many lands has the price been paid, in many lands shall it yet be paid.

"Now will I deal with the Fox and the Bear. It seems they have cast eyes upon the maiden. So? Behold, I have bought her! Thling-Tinneh leans upon the rifle; the goods of purchase are by his fire. Yet will I be fair to the young men. To the Fox, whose tongue is dry with many words, will I give of tobacco five long plugs. Thus will his mouth be wetted that he may make much noise in the council. But to the Bear, of whom I am well proud, will I give of blankets two; of flour, twenty cups; of tobacco, double that of the Fox; and if he fare with me over the mountains of the East, then will I give him a rifle, mate to Thling-Tinneh's. If not? Good! The Wolf is weary of speech. Yet once again will he say the Law: "Whoso taketh the life of one Wolf, the forfeit shall ten of his people pay."

Mackenzie smiled as he stepped back to his old position, but at heart he was full of trouble. The night was yet dark. The girl came to his side, and he listened closely as she told of the Bear's battle-tricks with the knife.

The decision was for war. In a trice, scores of moccasins were widening the space of beaten snow by the fire. There was much chatter about the seeming defeat of the Shaman; some averred he had but withheld his power, while others conned past events and agreed with the Wolf. The Bear came to the center of the battleground, a long naked hunting knife of Russian make in his hand. The Fox called attention to Mackenzie's revolvers; so he stripped his belt, buckling it about Zarinska, into whose hands he also intrusted his rifle. She shook her head that she could not shoot—small chance had a woman to handle such precious things.

"Then, if danger come by my back, cry aloud, 'My husband!' No, thus: 'My husband!' "

He laughed as she repeated it, pinched her cheek, and re-entered the circle. Not only in reach and stature had the Bear the advantage of him, but his blade was longer by a good two inches. "Scruff" Mackenzie had looked into the eyes of men before, and he knew it was a man who stood against him; yet he quickened to the glint of light on the steel, to the dominant pulse of his race.

Time and again he was forced to the edge of the fire or the deep snow, and time and again, with the foot tactics of the pugilist, he worked back to the center. Not a voice was lifted in encouragement, while his antagonist was heartened with applause, suggestions and warnings. But his teeth only shut the tighter as the knives clashed together, and he thrust or eluded with a coolness born of conscious strength. At first he felt compassion for his enemy; but this fled before the primal instinct of life, which in turn gave way to the lust of slaughter. The ten thousand years of culture fell from him, and he was a cave-dweller, doing battle for his female.

Twice he pricked the Bear, getting away unscathed; but the third time caught, and to save himself, free hands closed on fighting hands, and they came together. Then did he realize the tremendous strength of his opponent. His muscles were knotted in painful lumps, and cords and tendons threatened to snap with the strain; yet nearer and nearer came the Russian steel. He tried to break away, but only weakened himself. The fur clad circle closed in, certain of and anxious to see the final stroke. But with wrestler's trick, swinging partly to the side, he struck at his adversary with his head. Involuntarily the Bear leaned back, disturbing his center of gravity. Simultaneously with this, Mackenzie tripped properly and threw his whole weight forward, hurling him clear through the circle into the deep snow. The Bear floundered out and came back full tilt.

"O my husband!" Zarinska's voice rang out, vibrant with danger.

To the twang of a bow-string, Mackenzie swept low to the ground, and a bone-barbed arrow passed over him into the breast of the Bear, whose momentum carried him over his crouching foe. The next instant Mackenzie was up and about. The Bear lay motionless, but across the fire was the Shaman, drawing a second arrow.

Mackenzie's knife leaped short in the air. He caught the heavy blade by the point. There was a flash of light as it spanned the fire. Then the Shaman, the hilt alone appearing without his throat, swayed a moment and pitched forward into the glowing embers.

Click! click!—the Fox had possessed himself of Thling-Tinneh's rifle and was vainly trying to throw a shell into place. But he dropped it at the sound of Mackenzie's laughter.

"So the Fox has not learned the way of the plaything? He is yet a woman. Come! Bring it, that I may show thee!"

The Fox hesitated.

"Come, I say!"

He slouched forward like a beaten cur.

"Thus, and thus; so the thing is done."

A shell flew into place, and the trigger was at cock as Mackenzie brought it to shoulder.

"The Fox has said great deeds were afoot this night, and he spoke true. There have been great deeds, yet least among them were those of the Fox. Is he still intent to take Zarinska to his lodge? Is he minded to tread the trail already broken by the Shaman and the Bear? No? Good!"

Mackenzie turned and drew his knife from the priest's throat.

"Are any of the young men so minded? If so, the Wolf will take them by two and three till none are left. No? Good! Thling-Tinneh, I now give thee this rifle a second time. If, in the days to come, thou shouldst journey to the Country of the Yukon, know thou that there shall always be a place and much food by the fire of the Wolf. The night is now passing into the day. I go, but I may come again. And for the last time remember the Law of the Wolf!"

He was supernatural in their sight as he rejoined Zarinska. She took her place at the head of the team, and the dogs swung into motion. A few moments later they were swallowed up by the ghostly forest. Till now Mackenzie had waited; he slipped into his snow-shoes to follow.

"Has the Wolf forgotten the five long plugs?"

Mackenzie turned upon the Fox angrily; then the humor of it struck him.

"I will give thee one short plug."

"As the Wolf sees fit," meekly responded the Fox, stretching out his hand.

Personal Qualities of Jack London

By John D. Barry

IT WAS terrible about Jack London, wasn't it?" said the barber, as I leaned back in his chair.

"Did you know him?" I asked.

"I've known him for years. Whenever he was staying near here for a few days he'd drop in, generally every day. He was always in a rush, and he never let me shave him more than once over. It was funny when I was cutting his hair to see how particular he was. He wanted it done just so; not fancy, you know, but rough. He didn't want to look fussed up. I guess he had a way of his own. Gee, but how he did enjoy himself. He had a good time every minute. When he was here he was always telling stories and talking about that ranch of his. He wanted me to go up some day and see it."

Those words were characteristic of much of the talk going on about Jack London since his death. After his success, when he might have become conventional and confine himself to the paths of the conventional, he remained independent and free. He enjoyed the wide variety of his contacts. The man in the street he met with as much pleasure as the great ones of the earth that he was privileged to know in his years of prosperity, often with much more pleasure. For he had his moments of embarrassment. There were people that could afflict him with their over-refinement and their importance. He liked best to be among those he could be on equal terms with, bursting into loud talk and laughter.

And yet he enjoyed being quiet, too. His love of retirement and peace were among the forces that led him away from the life of cities, where he might have been a great figure, into the comparative solitude of the country. But he could not escape being a great figure everywhere. "He will be missed in the Valley of the Moon," said one of his friends, who had long had him for a neighbor. "He was a big influence there. His enterprise and energy were an inspiration to the whole valley."

Socialist as he was, lover of democracy, democrat not only in his theories but in his feeling as well, Jack London enjoyed being the possessor of a great domain. He took pleasure in sitting on his high cart and driving a string of horses through gateway after gateway, his round, boyish face glowing under his gray felt sombrero. Some day he expected to reap a great harvest from the thousands of eucalyptus trees that he had planted there. He took delight in watching their growth.

Like many literary men, he had a fondness for reading aloud. His own stories he read in a way that was attractive on account of its spontaneity and freedom from self-consciousness. Better than his own stories he liked to read the verses of George Sterling. When I last saw him he spoke with enthusiasm of the lyrics that Sterling had been writing, remarkable for their simplicity and grace of diction and for their delicacy of thought and feeling.

If Jack London had been given his way in the writing of fiction, he would not have devoted himself so much to adventure. He was greatly drawn to those psychological themes that had a special interest for a few readers and no interest whatsoever for the multitude. Now and then he would venture on this forbidden ground, only to find that some of his warmer admirers among magazine editors, would become obdurate. Even at the height of his fame he wrote short stories that could not get into the magazines and that he could get to the public only between the covers of a book.

So far as the drama was concerned, he used to say that he had never had any luck. Other writers would often ask for permission to dramatize his stories, and several of them succeeded in getting dramatic versions on the stage. But none of them greatly prospered. When moving pictures became popular it looked as if, among contemporary American writers, Jack London would reap the richest harvest. And he might have been wonderfully successful if the moving picture rights of his stories had been more adroitly marketed. Many fine pictures were made from his work, and they were seen by hundreds of thousands; but what the author derived from them consisted largely of vexatious law suits.

There probably never was a more photographed author than Jack London. He took boyish delight in seeing himself reproduced in a vast number of poses. Visitors at his ranch on leaving, if they expressed an interest in photographs, were likely to go away with a half dozen or more in their pockets. His closest friends have photographs of him in scant costume, or no costume at all, taken for the purpose of displaying his extraordinary muscular development. The lifetime of roughing it had given him a physique that seemed capable of resisting any kind of attack, and yet he subjected himself to ways of living that were too much, even for his vitality. Of those ways he spoke himself with greatest frankness in his autobiographical books.

In spite of his claim that he did not like the kind of writing he had to do to make money, Jack London nevertheless enjoyed the literary career in itself, and all that it brought in the way of interest and friends. But when his day's work was done he did not wish to bother over it again. He was very different from those writers who were continually revising. The reading of proof he regarded as a great bore, and he was glad to have friends whose judgment he trusted take the burden off his mind. Some of his books he would allow to go before the public without looking over them in type.

Are There Any Thrills Left in Life?

By Jack London

When I lie on the placid beach at Waikiki, in the Hawaiian Islands, as I did last year, and a stranger introduces himself as the person who settled the estate of Captain Keeler; and when that stranger explains that Captain Keeler came to his death by having his head chopped off and smoke-cured by the cannibal head-hunters of the Solomon Islands in the West South Pacific; and when I remember back through the several brief years, to when Captain Keller, a youth of 22 and master of the schooner Eugenie, was sailed deep with me on many a night, and played poker to the dawn, and took hasheesh with me for the entertainment of the wild crew of Penduffryn; and who, when I was wrecked on the outer reef of Malu, on the island of Malaita, with 1,500 naked Bushmen and head-hunters on the beach armed with horse-pistols, Snider rifles, tomahawks, spears, war-clubs and bows and arrows, and with scores of war-canoes, filled with salt-water head-hunters and man-eaters holding their place on the fringe of the breaking surf alongside of us, only four whites of us, including my wife, on board—when Captain Keller burst through the rain-squalls to windward, in a whale-boat, with a crew of negroes, himself rushing to our rescue, bare-footed and bare-legged, clad in loin-cloth and six-penny undershirt, a brace of guns strapped about his middle—I say, when I remember all this, that adventure and romance are not dead as I lie on the placid beach of Waikiki.

Recollections of the Late Jack London

By Edgar Lucien Larkin

ON SEPTEMBER 13, 1906, I spent a night at Jack London's home in Sonoma. The house was crowded with guests. Jack took me to the place he had chosen for me . . .

Jack opened the door of his den, bade me enter, and pointed to a huge arm chair. He lighted up, said a few pleasant words, opened a door looking into the other half of the building, showed me his bed, bade me goodnight. And when all alone I tore up things in an exploration exercise. I was in one of the greatest literary centers of the world. The working table was wide and long. It was heaped up with an incredible stock of writing paper of varying sizes, pens by the gross, pencils, not one well sharpened, quart bottles of ink, sheets of postage stamps and the like.

But see these things, stories almost finished, others half, a third or fourth written; tense, exceedingly dramatic humanity plots and plans of other writings; sketches for illustrations of books, highly ideal, letters in heaps from all parts of the world and from many publishers.

I was glad there was no room for me in the house.

* * *

There! I heard a sweetly sad and solemn bell, tuneful bell, then another, and soon another, no two sounding the same note. But they had been attuned by a master of harmonics. They were three sacred Korean temple service bells secured when Mr. London was Russian-Japanese war correspondent. They had been fastened to twigs. The well known "Valley of the Moon" breeze, just in from the ocean, swayed the branches and rang them with delicate, excessively harmonic notes. But I didn't know they were there.

Finally a gust caused one to strike the window pane. I explored and solved this apparently esoteric mystery. Esoteric, indeed, for the bells had been in use, maybe, for centuries, in archaic Asiatic mysteries greater than those of Eleusis in Greece.

* * *

On a shelf across a corner above the chairback I counted thirteen books. I arose and took them down, one by one, looked at their dates. They had all been written by Mr. London within five years. He was born in San Francisco on January 12, 1876. I was looking them over at 1 a. m., September 14, 1906. Go do this work, and you will begin to sense the true meaning of the word work.

There were Mr. London's Arctic and Klondike outfits, curios from Asia and many things belonging to his dogs for their comfort in cold.

No matter where the reader of these lines may be, it is an honor for him to love our brothers, the animals, as did their well known friend Jack. Do you suppose for an instant that Jack London would rise, brace himself and then jerk and twist steel bits against quivering flesh, the mouths of his beloved horses?

Here I was in a world of pure literature—story, drama—these that rock the soul like the rocking of a baby's cradle. I could not wait longer. I seized Jack's pen and a lot of paper at 1:40 and "wrote a piece" for the Examiner, which was published a few days later. Then to Jack's bed at 3:15 a. m.

Jack London's Resignation from the Socialist Party

Honolulu, March 7, 1916.

Glen Ellen,
    Sonoma County, California.

Dear Comrades:

I am resigning from the Socialist Party, because of its lack of fire and fight, and its loss of emphasis on the class struggle.

I was originally a member of the old revolutionary, up-on-its-hind-legs, fighting, Socialist Labor Party. Since then, and to the present time, I have been a fighting member of the Socialist Party. My fighting record in the Cause is not, even at this late date, already entirely forgotten. Trained in the class struggle, as taught and practiced by the Socialist Labor Party, my own highest judgment concurring, I believed that the working class, by fighting, by never fusing, by never making terms with the enemy, could emancipate itself. Since the whole trend of Socialism in the United States during recent years has been one of peaceableness and compromise, I find that my mind refuses further sanction of my remaining a party member. Hence my resignation.

Please include my comrade wife, Charmian K. London's, resignation with mine.

My final word is that liberty, freedom and independence are royal things that cannot be presented to, nor thrust upon, races or classes. If races and classes cannot rise up and by their strength of brain and brawn, wrest from the world liberty, freedom and independence, they never in time can come to these royal possessions . . . and if such royal things are kindly presented to them by superior individuals, on silver platters, they will know not what to do with them, will fail to make use of them, and will be what they have always been in the past . . . inferior races and inferior classes.

Yours for the Revolution,

JACK LONDON.

Mrs. Jack London's "Log of the Snark"

By Beatrice Langdon

IN THE absence of other lengthy biography of Jack London, Mrs. London's "Log of the Snark" serves well, for she has given us an intimate study of her husband in the day-to-day life of their remarkable adventure. One learns of Jack's disposition, his habits of work and play, in a way that would be impossible for any one but his hourly companion to handle. The book is full of intimate touches that picture the exuberant Jack in all his variety.

Their union was ideal, each constantly striving to find some more endearing term to confer on the other. Jack had a shower of names to which he was everlastingly adding—"The "Skipper's Sweetheart," "Jack's Wife," "Mate Woman," "Mate," "Crackerjack," "Pal." She showered him with as many. Their exuberant enthusiasm, vitality and spontaneity kept pace with the dancing hours. Everything was a delight, especially adventure, a word they both spelled in huge capital letters. All this is set forth in Charmion London's "Log of the Snark," her first book. The way it came to be written "was mostly due to Jack. Be it known that he detests letter writing, although a more enthusiastic recipient of correspondence never slit an envelope. When I decided to keep a typewritten diary of the voyage to be circulated in lieu of individual letters, my husband hailed the scheme with delight."

The Snark measured fifty-seven feet over all, with a fifteen foot beam, drawing six feet and fifty tons of metal on her beam. Friends of the Londons suggested such names as "Petrel," "Sea Bird," "White Wings" and "Sea Wolves," but Jack and Charmian, with a higher flight of imagination, settled on "The Snark," so happily invented by Lewis Carroll. The vessel was planned in 1905. But the great fire in San Francisco in the following year upset the work, and the vessel was finally completed, April 25, 1907. So gallant a little craft deserved some consideration, but the contractors had their own opinion on this score. London had naturally specified for the best materials to be had. Later it was discovered that inferior supplies had been used, with the result that several times the lives of the voyagers were imperiled during heavy storm stress, and were saved only by Jack's splendid seamanship and ingenuity.

The happy adventurers passed through the Golden Gate, outward bound, on April 25, 1907 sighting Maui May 17. At Pearl Harbor they spent a month of delight at Hilo (Hawaiian Islands), a month of vexatious delay for engine repairs, weaknesses that had developed during the trip from San Francisco. Crossing the line, November 30th, they sighted land in the Marquesas, December 6th, to the profit of Jack. He had wagered with a fellow voyager who declared they would not reach Nuva-Hiva by Dec. 12. They made Tahiti April 5, and entered Pago Pago harbor, May 3. That same month they touched at Apia, Samoa and Savaii. From the Fijis they sailed to the New Hebrides, reaching Fort Resolution, June 11th. In July they became the guests of the owner of the Pennduffryn Plantation, Island of Guadalcanal, Solomon Islands. There they spent several weeks before resuming the progress from island to island. It was during this period of the voyage that Jack began to show signs of serious illness. The malady manifested itself by intense burning in the skin, due, it was thought, to the nervousness experienced in whipping the Snark into sailing shade.

He and Mate discussed the situation. Jack declared that if he could slip back to his home in the Valley of the Moon, California, he would be able to pull himself together with a rush. And he did. The party went to Sydney, Australia, and took passage to California. They had planned to be gone seven years, and, because of Jack's sudden illness, returned in eighteen months.

Up to almost the last minute, the skipper and the skipper's wife, exuberant with life and adventure, never met a dull day. There were games of cribbage and poker, much writing and reading, and family boxing matches. (Mrs. Jack is an experienced boxer, tutored early by her husband.) They fished for dolphin, bonita and shark, and used baited hooks, harpoon and rifle shot at the larger fish. They slept on the deck in the beautiful tropic moonlight, took their trick at the watches at the wheel, and stood by in gales and in patching recalcitrant machinery. The crew of half a dozen found only exhilaration in everything about them.

Charmian London in her diary sets out all this in intimate form, even to the sea she learned to know so well:

"The sea is not a lovable monster. And monster it is. It is beautiful, the sea, always beautiful in one way or another; but it is cruel and unmindful of life that is in it and upon it. It was cruel last evening, in the lurid, low sunset that made it glow, dully to the cold, mocking ragged moonrise that made it look like death. The waves positively beckoned when they arose and pitched toward our boat laboring in the trough. And all the long night it seemed to me that I heard voices through the planking, talking, talking aimlessly, monotonously, querulously; and I couldn't make out whether it was the ocean calling from the out-side of the ship, herself muttering gropingly, finding herself. If the voices are of the ship, they will soon cease, for she must find herself. But if they are the voices of the sea, they must be sad sirens that cry, restlessly, questioning, unsatisfied, quaint, homeless little sirens.

* * *

"Jack enticed me out to the tip end of the bowsprit, with a heavy sea rolling. I must frankly admit that I felt shaky climbing out, with my feet on a stell-stay only a few inches above the crackling foam, and my hands clinging to the lunging spar. But it was wonderful to watch the yacht swing magnificently over the undulating blue hills, now one side hulled in the rushing, dazzling smother, now the other, the sunshot turquoise water rolling back from the shining, cleaving bows, and mixing with the milky froth pressed under. Now the man at the wheel would be far, far below us, sliding down that same mountain. But he never overtook us, for about that time we were raising our feet from the wet into which we had been plunged, and were holding on for dear life as the Snark's doughty forefoot pawed another steep rise."

* * *

At Tahae in the Marquesas the travelers, on renting the only available cottage, were happy to find that it was the old clubhouse where Stevenson frequently dropped in on his visits to that place. The Marquesas women's looks were disappointing to the white women, but the race has not been improving since the far off days when Norman Melville called them the fairest and handsomest women of the South Sea islanders. There was feasting in honor of the Snark's advent: calabashes of poi-poi, made from bread fruit, where the Hawaiians use taro; and purke (pig)—fourteen huge cocoanut-fed hogs roasted whole in ovens of hot stones. The barbaric music was up to all expectations, and there was dancing not to be found fault with by seekers of the outlandish. The procession to the feast supplied a "vivid, savage picture." One man wore a silk hat and a "tattered rag of a calico shirt;" there were several battered derbys, and the king's son wore ducks and a straw hat. The hula-hula was danced to the music of an accordion. And when Mrs. London visited the vai, she mourned; Melville saw it blooming and happy, now it is unwholesome, the remnant of the people ragged in civilized calico, and wretched. But in Ho-o-umi Valley the explorers found "a little vale that looks as Typpe must have looked in her hey-day," a bit of aboriginal fairyland. Here was a "prospect of plenty." Rich lands border the stream that threads the valley, breadfruit, bananas and cocoanut palms thrive. Copperskinned natives fish in the river. Grass huts, "the quintessence of savage picturesqueness," dot the landscape. In the little village at the mouth of the valley the explorers met "a Marquesan Adonis," a lithe, strong specimen of manhood, whose memory they cherish as of the approximation to the Typean of older chronicles.

Going into Papeete, after being saluted by the U. S. Cruiser Annapolis, the Snarkers were hailed from a native craft flying a red flag. Standing, in the canoe, was "a startling Biblical figure," a tall, tawny blonde man, clad only in a sleeveless shirt of large mesh fishnet and a scarlet loin cloth. "Hulloa, Jack; hulloa, Charmian!" It was astonishing. Suddenly they recognized him as a friend last met in California, some years before, and whom they called the "Nature Man."

"What's the red flag for?" asked London.

"Socialism, of course."

"Oh, I know that; but what are you doing with it?"

"Delivering the message," and the flag-bearer made a sweeping gesture towards Papeete.

"To Tahiti?" asked London, incredulously.

"Sure."

The Nature Man brought better things to his white friends than to his dusky proteges, for he left aboard the Snark a basket filled with clear white honey, two ripe mangoes, cocoanut cream and alligator pears.

* * *

And Mrs. Jack London goes on with her narrative:

"I am writing at a little greentopped table on which lie my fiveshooter and a Winchester automatic rifle containing eleven cartridges. Outside is an intermittent gale of wind, thrashing the banyans and palms, whipping the breakers into hoarse, coarse roaring, varied by blasts of thunder and lightning of all descriptions; and through the clamor I can just catch the pulling-calls of desperately hauling men on yacht and reef, as they work to clear the vessel at high water . . . I hear no shots, and am fairly certain our crowd is not being annoyed by the scoundrelly maneaters ashore. I am not exactly happy with my man out there, tired and anxious and supperless; and the yacht, in spite of almost unbelievable staunchness, may break up in the night. They could get away in the whaleboats —but what would they meet if they tried to land on the beach—the savages knowing the ship had been deserted!"

* * *

"Jack has just finished a beautiful South Sea story, entitled 'The Heathen,' and is now deep in a novel, 'Adventure,' with the stage of action right here on Pennduffryn Mountains. Besides our steady work these past three weeks and over, we have boxed, ridden horseback and swum at sunset, sometimes in tropical showers when the palms lay against the stormy sky like green enamel on a slate background, with ever an eye for alligators."

Mrs. Jack called Jack's work "Two hours of creation a day." Jack vilified the stunt by dubbing it "bread and butter."

* * *

All very fascinating is this record of voyaging in the South Seas. It was in these same Solomon Islands that the greatest adventure befell the party. Some of the inhabitants in the interior still reflect the avatism of their forebears, and are charged with being head-hunters and cannibals. Danger signs, in landing in such places, by no means passed with the day of Captain Cook; there is an added nuisance: some of these islanders now carry rifles with soft-nosed bullets. A fact which explains that Mrs. Jack London, while in that locality, slept with a rifle by her side and carried a revolver in her holster by day. Jack found occasion to give a little exhibition of quick firing with an automatic pistol, just to impress the natives.

It was in this situation that the party one day heard the news of the murder of friends near by, Claud Bernays of the Penduffryn Mountain Plantation, and Captain Keller of the ship Eugenie. Jack made a note of this cannibalism in order to meet in this country the attacks of certain critics who derided his "realistic" stories of the South Seas regarding cannibalism and other forms of murder. Since then other authentic cases have come to light to fortify Jack London's position.

And what of the good ship, "The Snark?" She was sold "for a fraction of her cost," estimated at $25,000, to an English syndicate, and handily was used by them for trading purposes in the New Hebrides. Later the Londons heard of her in the Bering Sea, off Alaska, and later still they met friends who had been aboard her at Kodiak, Alaska, in 1911. In 1912, she was reported to have donned a coat of new green paint and was harboring around Seattle. The Londons had reached that city a short time before, from a five months' wind-jamming voyage from Baltimore around Cape Horn, and had left just before the Snark reached Seattle.

In whatever part of the Seven Seas "The Snark" may poke her adventurous nose she is certain to make history, for it was written all over her during her planning, building and the extraordinary experiences she gave the Londons and their friends in the adventurous South Seas, as is most entertainingly set forth by Mrs. Jack London in her "Log" of that vessel.

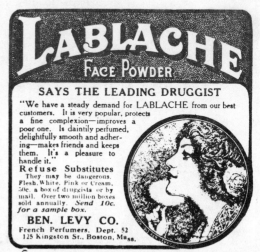

Miss Hamlin's School For Girls

Home Building on Pacific Avenue
of Miss Hamlin's School for Girls

Boarding and day pupils. Pupils received at any time. Accredited by all accrediting institutions, both in California and in Eastern States. French school for little children. Please call, phone or address

MISS HAMLIN

TELEPHONE WEST 546

2230 PACIFIC AVENUE   2117 } **BROADWAY**
                            2123

SAN FRANCISCO, CAL.

GET 6 NEW SUBSCRIBERS
TO OVERLAND MONTHLY
===== AND =====

Receive a MANDEL-ETTE CAMERA, the new one minute photographic creation, the latest thing in cameras.

The Mandel-ette takes and finishes original post-card photographs in one minute without plates or films. No printing; no dark rooms; no experience required. Press the button, and the Mandel-ette turns out three completed pictures in one minute. It embodies a camera, developing chamber, and dark room all in one— a miniature photograph gallery, reducing the cost of the ordinary photograph from 10 cents to 1½ cents. The magazine holds from 16 to 50 2½x3½ post cards, and can be loaded in broad day-light; no dark room necessary. Simple instructions accompany each camera.

A child can take perfect pictures with it.

Price on the market, $5.

OVERLAND MONTHLY for one year and a Mandel-ette Camera, $5.
Get 6 NEW SUBSCRIBERS for OVERLAND MONTHLY, and forward the subscriptions and $9.00, and you will receive a Mandel-ette Camera FREE.

Address, OVERLAND MONTHLY
259 Minna Street, San Francisco

"HIS MASTER'S VOICE"

Every kind of music for everybody

Your kind of music for you! The kind of music you like best!

Do you prefer to hear magnificent operatic arias, portrayed by Caruso or Farrar or Melba? Or are your favorites the charming old songs of yesteryear—the ballads so sweetly sung by Gluck and McCormack?

Or it may be that your tastes run to instrumental solos—the exquisite renditions of Elman or Kreisler or Paderewski. Then again, perhaps, you would rather hear Sousa's Band play some of his own stirring marches, or enjoy Harry Lauder's inimitable witticisms.

No matter—you can hear them all on the Victrola. It is supreme in all fields of musical endeavor. It is *the* instrument for every home.

Hear your favorite music today at any Victor dealer's. He will gladly play any music you wish to hear, and demonstrate the various styles of the Victor and Victrola —$10 to $400.

Victor Talking Machine Co.
Camden, N. J., U. S. A.
Berliner Gramophone Co., Montreal, Canadian Distributors

Important Notice. All Victor Talking Machines are patented and are only *licensed*, and with right of use with Victor Records only. All Victor Records are patented and are only *licensed*, and with right of use on Victor Talking Machines only. Victor Records and Victor Machines are scientifically coordinated and synchronized by our special processes of manufacture; and their use, except with each other, is not only unauthorized, but damaging and unsatisfactory.

"Victrola" is the Registered Trade-mark of the Victor Talking Machine Company designating the products of this Company only. **Warning:** The use of the word **Victrola** upon or in the promotion or sale of any other Talking Machine or Phonograph products is misleading and illegal.

Victrola XVII, $250
Victrola XVII, electric, $300
Mahogany or oak

Victrola